A

Tim Heald began his writing life as a
journalist but has also written a dozen
crime novels. His non-fiction books have
covered Old Boy networks, cricket
grounds and stately homes. His previous
biographies have been about the Duke
of Edinburgh and Denis Compton. His
next is a life of the broadcaster,
Brian Johnston.

A Life of Love

Barbara Cartland

TIM HEALD

Mandarin

A Mandarin Paperback
A LIFE OF LOVE

First published in Great Britain 1994
by Sinclair-Stevenson
This edition published 1995
by Mandarin Paperbacks
an imprint of Reed International Books Ltd
Michelin House, 81 Fulham Road, London SW3 6RB
and Auckland, Melbourne, Singapore and Toronto

All the illustrations in this book are reproduced
courtesy of the Hulton Deutsch Collection,
with the exception of the picture of Barbara in Tudor costume
on the third page of illustrations and the picture
of Barbara bearing books on the seventh page of illustrations,
which are reproduced courtesy of Popperfoto.

Copyright © 1994 by Tim Heald
The author has asserted his moral rights

A CIP catalogue record for this title
is available from the British Library
ISBN 0 7493 2089 3

Printed and bound in Great Britain
by Cox & Wyman Ltd, Reading, Berkshire

Chapter One

I meet Barbara when I am young. I am bowled over. The years pass. I decide to write a book about her. She seems pleased. We have trouble with publishers. Finally we find a good one. Barbara's son Ian comes to lunch. We begin work.

I first interviewed Barbara Cartland in 1967 when I was a twenty-three-year-old feature writer on the *Sunday Express*. My rather hackneyed idea was to compile a four-part series on 'People We Love to Hate'. These were to be 'The Traffic Warden', 'The Mother-in-Law', 'The Football Referee', and 'The Income Tax Inspector'. They were generic articles bolstered with quotations from real-life people, mostly anonymous.

My ostensible reason for approaching Barbara Cartland for the mother-in-law piece was that she had been the Earl of Dartmouth's mother-in-law for the past twenty-one years. This was, of course, a ridiculous pretext. The only reason for the Earl of Dartmouth having any public reputation was that he was sandwiched uncomfortably between two exceptionally formidable and forthright personalities: his wife, Raine, the Countess, and his mother-in-law, Barbara Cartland, the most prolific romantic novelist of her, or any other's, day. 'Personality' was the operative word. They were both larger than life and much larger than the poor Earl.

Barbara Cartland has always been adroit at public relations so it was not altogether surprising that I was invited to lunch at Camfield Place, her early nineteenth-century pile in stockbroker Hertfordshire. No question of being fobbed off with a few well-chosen words on the phone.

It was a good but intimidating lunch. I was in my early twenties and she in her late sixties and there were just the two of us. My most vivid memory is of the large quantity of silver on the table. A lot of silver pheasants and a tremendous sense of candelabra. I was also acutely nervous about my table manners. When, on my departure, she presented me with a signed copy of her *Etiquette Handbook* I felt I had failed the test.

On reflection, however, I like to think she gave it to me because of the section on 'Mothers-in-law'. In the 1990s the very idea of a book on etiquette has become laughable, the idea of one by Barbara Cartland even more so. Yet, thumbing through it, a quarter of a century later I am struck by the amount of sturdy good sense she talks. The initial premise, for instance: 'There is a lot of nonsense talked about etiquette. At bedrock the word really means good manners; and good manners are merely the evidence of man's civilisation.'

I suppose that's a thoroughly old-fashioned view and perhaps it's just because I'm now middle-aged that I find myself, more or less, agreeing. I rather warm to the sentiments, as well as to the pithy way she expresses them. Her former boss, Lord Beaverbrook, would have approved.

After lunch we adjourned to the drawing-room for the interview proper. As always she seems to have given me precisely the quotations I had come for just as she has always done for journalists of every description on what, even in her nineties, appears to be an almost hourly basis. Latterly such succinct pronouncements have become known, in deference to our television age, as 'soundbites'. She is a past-mistress of them.

The first line was 'I am a very good mother-in-law'.

This is a characteristic Cartlandism. She may not actually be as pleased with herself as she sometimes seems but she is certainly not going to say so in public. At the time I described this as 'disarming'. Not everyone finds it so. Maybe it's an oddity in myself, but I *do* find such assertive self-confidence disarming, not least because, to me, it suggests a deep uncertainty within. The truly self-confident person shrugs and smiles and invites you to take them or leave them. Not Dame Barbara.

She continued with brisk advice on the matter of mothers-in-law, much in line with that contained in her etiquette book, and of which, perhaps, more later. I dutifully wrote it down and it duly appeared in the *Express* together with a Giles cartoon, mothers-in-law being grist to Carl Giles's mill.

A day or so later a letter arrived from Miss Cartland which read, 'Thank you so very much for the kind things you say about me in your brilliantly written article. I enjoyed our lunch so much and I hope you will come again. All best wishes for what will obviously be a very, very successful career. Blessings . . .' The letter was handwritten and each of the three 'very's was underlined twice. Of course it was over the top but one couldn't, at twenty-three years old, fail to be flattered.

During the next quarter of a century our paths did not cross and I never did return to Camfield Place. I could hardly fail to be aware of her, however, because she seemed to crop up every day in the press or on radio and television and she strode into her nineties with her energy undiluted and her productivity undiminished. In 1981 her step-granddaughter, Lady Diana Spencer, married the Prince of Wales; by 1992 she had written 575 books thus becoming the world's most prolific author and surpassing the previous record holder, John Creasey. The media found her irresistible for she could

5

be relied on for a forthright opinion on practically anything from AIDS to whether or not ladies should ride side-saddle. In 1991 she was made a Dame.

In 1991 I published a biography of the Duke of Edinburgh and was looking for someone else to write about. What made the Duke of Edinburgh an interesting subject for a book, and a commercial one as well, was not just that he was famous in this country and abroad, but that at the same time he seemed to have been quite adroit at concealing much of his true self from the public. He was one of those comparatively rare people who was almost universally familiar but about whom the first question was nearly always 'What's he *really* like?' He had enjoyed a long and full life, known interesting people, done interesting things, was known to a huge number of people and yet remained quite elusive and enigmatic.

I felt that Barbara Cartland came into this unusual category as well. She clearly has a high international profile. She is also a brilliant self-publicist. Almost everyone has a vision of this extraordinary pink-clad figure with astonishing eye make-up who is not only a hugely successful romantic novelist but also the step-grandmother of the Princess of Wales, a champion of health foods and of the gypsies, a scourge of feminism, defender of traditional sexual morality and all-purpose aphorist – surely one of the most quoted figures in Britain if not the world.

Yet our image of her is almost entirely a picture of her own painting. Even the most expert analysts have failed to get under her skin. In 1991 for instance she appeared 'In the Psychiatrist's Chair' with Dr Anthony Clare. This BBC radio programme is famous for getting the most redoubtable and experienced interviewees, wittingly or not, to peel away the onion skins of their personality. Yet Dame Barbara succeeded in coming out almost entirely unscathed. When I asked her about this she said that she had known before the programme started exactly what she wanted to say and had been determined 'not to let him get a word in edgeways'. She succeeded triumphantly, even unfazed when he asked her about 'the Curse'.

'Not something we used to talk about in our day,' she says. 'But in my day we didn't even talk about going to the lavatory. Nowadays everyone does it all the time.' Innocence, purity and an aversion to the public discussion of sex are all an integral part of the Cartland persona.

As far as I could see there were two previous biographies of her. One, by Gwen Robyns, published in 1984, was described as 'Authorised'. The other, published five years earlier, was a slimmer volume by 'Henry Cloud', which is an alias for John Pearson who wrote highly successful and decently critical lives of Ian Fleming and the Kray brothers. It seemed to me that much had happened to Barbara Cartland in the years since these publications. Also they both lacked what I would describe as 'distance'. It was almost as if she might have written them herself. Later Gwen Robyns said she would rather not help me but John Pearson came to lunch and though he did not quite say so, and though he obviously liked her very much, it seemed plain that Dame Barbara had been allowed to take her pink pencil to his text.

Part of her fascination for me lies in the fact that she has chosen to present herself as a fluffy piece of romantic nonsense while, in real life, being a tough, single-minded professional. She is infinitely more of a Baroness Thatcher or Kate Adie than the candy-floss image which stares out from the pink-washed cover of her printed curriculum vitae. Or so I thought when I first contemplated writing a book about her. Everyone, myself included, seemed to take her at face value. And the face value, apparently propagated by herself, did her less than justice. It almost encouraged the intelligentsia and the chattering classes to sneer and patronise. Anyone with any literary pretensions at all always affected to despise her books. Yet, with a single exception of whom more later, no one I know has ever admitted to reading one of them. Their reputation is based on their publicity. Their reality is unknown to the sort of people who edit the literary pages of serious newspapers, yet they are read by millions all over the world.

Prince Philip is not an easy act to follow but I thought Dame Barbara would be worth pursuing. I therefore approached her to see if she would be prepared to help.

From the first she seemed to be flattered and intrigued. She read and enjoyed my biography of the Duke enough to give it an unsolicited encomium in the *Evening Standard* and to speak approvingly of it on the radio. She also started to send me material: four volumes of autobiography, all long out of print; the Gwen Robyns book – 'I'm fond of Gwen,' she remarked over the phone in January 1992, 'but she does go on rather'; several slim volumes of typewritten stuff bound in pink with ribbon – correspondence, notes on 'How I wish to be remembered', and so on; a slim – pink again – brochure giving a chronology; a full list of her novels; her *Guiness Book of Records* entries and a page announcing her Investiture as a Dame.

We talked on the telephone. She said that her son, Ian, who manages her business affairs, was reluctant to have another book written about her. I wasn't altogether sure why. The ostensible reason was that there was nothing new to say, though I suspect he was nervous of harsh judgement and unwelcome disclosure. She took the line that she was worth a good book and that she would rather it were done in her lifetime so that she could, if necessary, 'put a stop to any nonsense'. And although she referred to Prince Philip more than once in disparaging terms she was clearly pleased with the idea that someone who had got reasonably close to *him* thought that *she* was also worth taking time and trouble over.

On 28 October 1991, I went to see her at home, for afternoon tea. One postponement was due, characteristically, to the fact that she had to attend Jean Rook's memorial service. They had a lot in common: the *Daily Express* (she was a Beaverbrook protégée before time began), flamboyance, vulgarity, certainty (even if only superficial).

She was in pink as usual but it was the eyelashes that struck me most forcibly – streaked silver-grey with what appeared to be a line of feathers growing out of them, like the band of JR's stetson in 'Dallas'. She appeared slightly deaf but couldn't be bothered with her hearing aid; and her sight was poor. However, she was unstoppably talkative and in full possession of her marbles. She was obviously having trouble with staff, though I sensed that she was the sort of employer who always had trouble with staff and yet inspired considerable, if sometimes grudging, loyalty. I was reminded of my one-time employer, Randolph Churchill, in this respect. 'Those women,' she said of her secretaries. I was surprised, but realised that she has a slightly self-conscious phobia about other women and also that she swears mildly but regularly. She admitted to 'brain fag' and put this down to the fact that already that day she had dictated 6,900 words of her latest novel to one of the long-suffering secretaries.

As this was an exploratory meeting I took no notes. She was riveting about 'Dickie' Mountbatten; how difficult some of his relations were; how she had to buy his shirts and a tea-set; how amazingly stupid and middle class this parliament was; how when (Princess) Margaret came to lunch she had told her this and told her that; what she said to the Prince of Wales; how the Queen treated Princess Michael. And there was a gargantuan tea in the dining-room with a huge cake and meringues and elegant cucumber sandwiches. The Pekinese and a black labrador called 'Dickie', after Mountbatten, got cake too. And for me there was also a wrapped present – one of her books, a diary of royal life – tied with the inevitable pink ribbon. I even got a kiss on departure.

It seemed clear that she wanted a 'proper' book. By this I understood her to mean something substantial, researched, documented and serious. Not dull or ponderous but considered. To help with this she would talk – incessantly but also revealingly and amusingly. She struck me as good already on Beaverbrook, Churchill and Mountbatten and, of course, on herself.

She had also kept endless papers and letters and evidently there would be no problem in having access to them.

I clearly wanted to talk to friends, colleagues, family and acquaintances and all manner of people who had known her. Obviously many are now dead but because she has remained so active there were still younger people around with lots to offer. And even if I didn't read them all I would have to examine the books and attempt some sort of textual analysis, as well as finding out why such unlikely people as Colonel Gaddafy and the Bulgarians are such passionate fans.

As she is quick to admit she has written a great deal about herself but self-portraits are not always revealing, at least not overtly so. I was anxious to get an outsider's perspective, to maintain some sort of distance and objectivity. Of course, I would be going over some familiar ground but I hoped to do so in a different way. The wedding-dress story for example. During the last war she decided, characteristically, that it was unromantic for our girls to be married in khaki, blue or grey and launched one of her crusades to provide a suitable supply of white wedding dresses.

She has described the campaign herself but being her she takes it for granted and manages, almost, to make it dull.

She cannot quite see that it is both wonderful and absurd, elevating and quixotic and quintessentially 'her'. To her it seems the most normal thing in the world so she tells it like that. No self-respecting third party could do the same.

Here, of course, lay danger. When I was writing about Prince Philip I agreed to let him and his staff see the manuscript in draft so that they could correct matters of fact. This led to prolonged dispute. It was settled amicably enough in the end but there were, inevitably, heated arguments about what constituted a fact, about who were reliable witnesses, whether or not a third-party opinion could be quoted, and so on. There were times when I felt the Palace were trespassing on my rights as author of the book and where I had to ask them to back off. Style and vocabulary, punctuation and construction, were, I felt, none of their business.

My heart sank, therefore, when Dame Barbara phoned and, without any preamble, asked, 'What are we going to do about your paragraphs?'

I did not like the use of the word 'we'. Nor did I know what she meant about my paragraphs.

'They're far too long,' she continued, without giving me a serious chance to answer the question. 'Dear Lord Beaverbrook always taught me that no paragraph should ever be more than three lines long. Your paragraphs are much too long. Nobody could possibly get to the end of them. Now are you going to be able to write short paragraphs?'

I felt, quite strongly, that my paragraphs were my affair and that the only person I was prepared to discuss them with was my editor. However I did not feel that it would be politic to say so, and certainly not at this still relatively early stage in my relationship with the Dame.

I therefore murmured something relatively non-committal to the effect that I too had served time with the *Daily Express* when it was still in the hands of the Aitken family (though

Lord Beaverbrook himself had passed on). It was quite true that there was a house rule about short paragraphs. Sentences too, come to that. My very first feature elicited an editorial complaint about an 'overlong' sentence. But a book and the *Daily Express* are not exactly the same thing.

My tactic during this, and indeed all, conversations with the Dame, was to say as little as possible. On the whole this was not difficult and a judicious grunt or 'Mmmm' accompanied with smiles and nods when actually in her presence seemed, more or less, to do the trick. She is a better talker than listener and requires minimal prompting.

I had heard, however, that – being a professional – she invariably insisted on a signed agreement even for the shortest interview. My friend Andrew Duncan, author of a weekly piece in the *Sunday Express Magazine* called 'Out to lunch', took Dame Barbara for a meal at her favourite Claridge's Hotel and was obliged to sign an undertaking for her to have approval of his article before publication. He told me that the maddening thing was that she asked him to remove all the most revealing details – not ones that were hostile or unpleasant, but ones that seemed – to him at least – to make her seem more interesting and human. Andrew said, for example, that when talking about her late husband Dame Barbara wept. When, however, he showed her his manuscript she denied that she had done so. Andrew felt the brief tears showed her in a sympathetic light but the Dame expunged them from the record.

I was not interested in writing a salacious, intrusive, muck-raking biography, but nor was I prepared to connive at a thinly disguised autobiographical hagiography. As with the Duke of Edinburgh, I was concerned to get the facts right but not with producing a facile whitewash. And the Dame would truncate my paragraphs over my dead body.

There was another problem which surprised me. Every

time I mentioned the idea of a book about her to my friends and colleagues they reacted with enthusiasm. Everyone seemed to recognise her as a phenomenon and my anecdotal impression was that she was a subject of considerable public interest.

Publishers, however, were much less excited by the prospect. Indeed so lukewarm were they that early in 1992 I conceded defeat and wrote to Dame Barbara to say that I was giving up the idea.

'I quite understand,' she replied. 'The British are hopeless in selling books.'

I noted that she was assiduous in taking her own advice about the brevity of paragraphs.

'My son is just coming back from Poland,' she continued, 'having signed fantastic contracts with Poland, Austria, Czechoslovakia and Russia. This is all because I am moral.

'It is very exciting to think that the world has woken up at last in trying to end the Permissive Era.'

For a while that seemed to be the end of the matter. I was disappointed but not altogether surprised. British publishing, like so many things British, is bedevilled by the desire to seem smart and fashionable. This breeds an obsession with what one's peers and competitors are doing, coupled with an often unthinking intellectual snobbery. Barbara Cartland's books were hugely popular but not in literary or intellectual circles. She herself was an extraordinary person who had led an extraordinary life, but it was not one which the average denizen of what used to be called Bloomsbury found sympathetic or interesting. More fool them, I thought, and turned to other ideas.

In the autumn of 1992, however, I mentioned the idea to the publisher Christopher Sinclair-Stevenson and he expressed an interest both personal and professional. Mr Sinclair-Stevenson is widely regarded in the book trade as an anachronism who likes to indulge his personal tastes. These are often regarded by others as eccentric and old-fashioned. Like me, he found the idea of a book about Dame Barbara 'fun'. This was a word he used without any prompting from me and it had been at the back of my mind from the beginning. (For him, as for me, it remained *le mot juste* throughout the exercise.)

He also agreed with me that the world-wide sales of her books and her ubiquitous dominance of the media made her, *ipso facto*, of interest. Perhaps not to the 'chattering classes', but certainly to huge numbers of what, for want of a better term, are often described as 'ordinary people'.

Sinclair-Stevenson's father-in-law, Sir Derek Walker-Smith (later Lord Broxbourne) had been the Cartlands' local Member of Parliament and they had even had a wedding present from the great authoress – a pair of jewel-encrusted matchbox holders! This small piece of family history may not have weighed heavily in Sinclair-Stevenson's decision to commission the book, but I like to think it weighed.

Once we had agreed to go ahead I wrote to Dame Barbara to tell her the good news. She responded on 12 January 1993 in the morning on the phone. First a secretary's voice, faintly long suffering, telling me that she had Dame Barbara for me and then, without any pleasantries or preliminaries, that wonderfully unstoppable Cartland crackle. 'Now we must think of something different to say. We don't want the same old stuff.' Once again it was 'we' from the beginning. '*We* must think what we're going to do.' I suggested, in one of the rare breaks, that I had better get down to some hard reading. She agreed that I must look at her four autobiographies but when I touched on the estimated 575 novels she said, quite rattily, 'Oh, you don't want to read them – they're all the same.' I said nothing to this, but thought, privately, that this was the sort of judgement made by her enemies. It was not what she herself was supposed to say. It reminded me of the jeweller Gerald Ratner denigrating his own wares.

Eventually she rang off, leaving me under no illusions that she intended the book to be a joint enterprise with her fingerprints all over the body. I also knew perfectly well that if she was allowed to control it then the book was indeed dead before it began. However, she had still not insisted on the dreaded formal agreement. I had already mentioned it to Christopher Sinclair-Stevenson and we had agreed that under no circumstances would we sign away our rights as author and publisher. However, we would wait and see.

We did not have to wait long. Just over a week later a letter arrived from the Islington office of Cartland Promotions. It was from Dame Barbara's son, Ian McCorquodale, the one who had made such a successful foray to Poland the year before. It was a friendly, even effusive, letter. He thought the news was 'splendid' and was 'sure that it will be a very good biography'. There was, though, a catch. He went on: 'When biographies have been written about my Mother before, we would insist on an agreement for approval by her before the book was published. I am sure that you will have no objection to this and if you are happy to go ahead on this basis, please let me know and I can draw up an appropriate agreement.'

Of course I was not happy, but what are publishers for if not to shelter behind on occasions such as this? I wrote back to Mr McCorquodale saying that I was sure there would be no problem (I wasn't) but I didn't feel able to enter into any such agreement without Christopher Sinclair-Stevenson being involved. Christopher felt this was a suitable case for lunch but not, on this occasion with Dame Barbara. It would be better if it were just the three of us. Mr McCorquodale agreed that lunch was 'a splendid idea'. He felt certain that 'we can work out a *modus operandi* about the contents of the book and the involvement of my Mother'. I was pleased to notice that his letter to Sinclair-Stevenson was a 'Dear Christopher' . . . 'Yours sincerely Ian'; but I was disconcerted to see that the capital letter he gave the word 'Mother' was habitual and therefore presumably done on purpose. When I first saw it I had assumed it was a typo.

Lunch was agreed for 25 February.

In these days of designer-bottled mineral water and sandwiches at the desk, it is fashionable to dismiss the efficacy of lunch. This, however, turned out to be a thoroughly productive and useful meal. Mr McCorquodale phoned the restaurant to say that he would be late on account of heavy traffic between Islington and the Old Brompton Road but arrived minutes later looking remarkably like a younger male version of his mother, though in a dark pin-stripe suit with not a glimmer of pink about his person.

Negotiations such as this seldom follow a set formula and the sub-text is usually as important as what is actually said out loud. I talked about my encounters with the Dame so far and about earlier ones with Prince Philip.

Mr McCorquodale talked about the difficulties of selling his mother's novels in China, and of different operations in such unlikely countries as Bulgaria and Saudi Arabia. These were intriguing and, as the meal progressed, increasingly funny. I particularly liked the success in selling love and romance to the French. 'After all,' as he put it, 'they think they invented it.' In April he was escorting Dame Barbara to Paris where a major romantic offensive was being mounted at the Galeries Lafayette. This struck all three of us as both resourceful and humorous.

It seemed to me that his attitude towards his mother was much as any good son's should be towards a mother: dutiful but sometimes exasperated, loving but alive to certain foibles. He was obviously her greatest champion but could, at the same time, see the funny side of her. I made it clear for my part that I was impressed by Dame Barbara's energy and professionalism but that a hagiography would not serve any purpose.

Shortly before the coffee Mr McCorquodale raised the question we had come to thrash out. Yet just as he raised it so he dismissed it. He had heard enough and sensed enough to think that it would be possible to go ahead without seeking formal approval of a written text. He looked forward to co-operating with us. I, for my part, said that I was fundamentally well disposed and would do my best to paint a fair, honest and accurate portrait of his extraordinary mother. Christopher Sinclair-Stevenson announced, hand on heart, that he would not be prepared to publish anything less. But we all recognised that it would be both more and less than a thinly disguised ghosted autobiography.

And so we parted.

Next morning the phone rang and her secretary announced Dame Barbara . . .

My work had just begun.

Chapter Two

Barbara is born. She has a long family tree. After a family tragedy times are hard for her parents, Bertie and Polly. Barbara goes to school. There is a war on. Another tragedy occurs.

She was born at 11.40 p.m. on 9 July 1901 at Vectis Lodge, Edgbaston, the home of her paternal grandparents. Her mother, Polly, had a difficult labour which was not altogether surprising for she was a tiny creature and when her first child finally arrived she weighed in at eight and a quarter pounds. At one point the doctor was so concerned that he asked the father, Bertie, whether, in the event of a catastrophe, he should save mother or child.

'Damn the bloody child,' said Bertie. 'Save my wife.'

In the event the little girl was safely delivered although on her arrival the doctor's immediate reaction was to exclaim to the nurse, 'It's dead'. After a judicious slapping, however, the infant came to life and in due course was christened Mary Barbara Hamilton.

In later years there was some dispute about the year of her birth and a different year appeared in one reference book. This was picked on by her enemies as evidence of vanity. She herself dismissed it as nothing more significant than a clerical error by a secretary.

Her parents, she believes, would have preferred a boy.

Mary Barbara Hamilton Cartland was a child of her class and her times, which meant that she and her immediate family seem to have spent an inordinate time trying to keep up appearances. In later life the Cartland accent and speech patterns seemed contrived and anachronistic – 'gel' for 'girl', much use of the phrase 'd'you see?'. Her attitude to 'class' was similarly old-fashioned. In private at least she would use 'common' as a term of abuse. One of the reasons that so many ministers in the government were inadequate was that they were 'common'. So, of course, were most members of parliament. 'Common little men', in fact.

From the very first it was clear that 'common' was the one thing little Mary Barbara Cartland was not. For a start both sides of the family were extremely old and distinguished. In her little autobituary, 'How I wish to be remembered', she writes, 'The Cartlands are reported in ancient Chronicles as being in Lanarkshire, Scotland before AD 1200 . . . The name could possibly be of Norman origin and belongs to the eleventh century or even earlier.' Her mother's maiden name was Scobell. Of her antecedents she writes, 'The Scobell Family was one of the oldest Saxon families in existence – an ancestor was Sheriff of Devon in 1022.'

Apart from the reference to the eleventh century Sheriff, this strikes me as a little vague. Gwen Robyns, the 'authorised' Cartland biographer, identifies him as Thomas de Scobenhull, describes him as 'High Sheriff' and gives his date as 1032. Surely, I thought, some mistake. After all the Normans didn't arrive until over thirty years later. Dr Maurice Keen, the Oxford mediaevalist, says tentatively that 'Thomas de Scobenhull doesn't exactly sound like an Anglo-Saxon name: you'd expect something like Egnoth or Sexfrith'. His suspicion is that Dame Barbara and Miss Robyns might be a few hundred years out.

Whoever they were and wherever they came from, neither

the Cartlands nor the Scobells could be said to have left a tremendously strong imprint on English history. Neither appear in *Debrett's Great British Families* by Hugh Montgomery-Massingberd nor in *The British Aristocracy* by the same Massingberd and Mark Bence-Jones. 'It's all complete and utter bunkum,' says Massingberd. 'Thirty years ago, before the great genealogical revolution, all sorts of people were going around claiming to be able to trace their ancestry back before the Conquest, but now that it's become seriously scientific you can't do it. You're doing really well these days if you can trace your family back to about 1550.' Maurice Keen referred me to Sir Anthony Wagner's *English Genealogy*. Sir Anthony said that 'as far as I know the ancestry of two extant English families only, Arden and Berkeley, can be carried back to pre-Conquest Englishmen'. As Dr Keen says, 'he ought to know and Sir Frank Stenton confirms.' Wagner was Garter King of Arms and Stenton author of the Oxford History of the period.

The College of Arms in the person of Theo Mathew, the Windsor Herald, could find no pedigree in its official registers for Scobell extending any further than that recorded during the Heralds' Visitation of Devon in 1620. That was for a Vincent Scobell of Plymouth. Windsor Herald also sent me a page from the eighth edition of *Burke's Peerage* which included a pedigree of Scobell. This did indeed say that the Scobells were an old Devon family. It also confirms Dr Keen's suspicions by saying that a Thomas de Scobbahull (spellings of the name vary) was indeed Sheriff of Devon but not until the early 1290s.

'As for Cartland,' says Windsor Herald, 'I can find absolutely nothing.' There is nothing at the College of Arms in London but, as he says, 'that might be expected of a Scottish family'. However he also consulted the standard bibliographies, including Ferguson, who deals with Scottish families and there was nothing under Cartland. He concludes, 'The records of the matriculation of Arms at Lyon Office in Edinburgh start in 1673 and have been published until 1973. No person in Scotland named Cartland matriculated Arms during that time.'

Dame Barbara also claims to be connected to the Princess of Wales not just through her daughter Raine being married to the late Earl Spencer but also because her second husband, Hugh McCorquodale, was descended from William the Conqueror's great-grandfather, Rollo.

None of this would matter much if it were not for the fact that it has become a small but necessary part of her myth. It is difficult to be sure how and when the misapprehension arose, but it fits in with that part of her which seems determined to seem socially more exalted than her ancestry might really suggest. 'A man can be of gentle birth and a boor by nature,' she once wrote. 'He can be a miner or a dustman and yet be a great gentleman.' Yet part of her seems to have trouble accepting such an egalitarian concept. When the *Guardian* asked readers to send in examples of 'unashamed rudeness', J.B. O'Connor nominated Dame Barbara because, 'When asked in a radio interview if she thought the class barriers had broken down, she replied: "Of course they have, or I wouldn't be talking to someone like you." '

Her forebears emerge from the mists of history and come more sharply into focus during the nineteenth century. The Cartlands evidently came from Lanarkshire where there is a small town of that name. They moved south and first settled in Worcestershire where 'my Great-Grandfather had an Estate'. Then at some time around the beginning of the Industrial Revolution Great-Grandfather moved towards the big smoke and started a 'brass factory' (foundry?) near Birmingham.

The second son of the wealthy brass manufacturer, James

Cartland, became 'a great financier' who apparently twice turned down the offer of 'a Baronetcy and a Knighthood' and in 1890 built Vectis Lodge in Edgbaston, an exercise in Victorian Gothick with gables, turrets and one of the earliest telephones. In 1900, James and his wife Flora ('a direct descendant of Robert the Bruce') enjoyed an income of about £15,000. 'Where there's muck there's brass.' The Cartlands were rich, the Cartlands were successful but the Cartlands were trade.

Not so the Scobells. Dame Barbara's maternal grandparents lived in a twenty-five-bedroom mansion outside Redmarley in Worcestershire. She says that 'by Victorian standards it was a moderate-sized house'. It required eight indoor servants and four gardeners. There was also a three-hundred-acre estate. Grandfather Scobell sounds like a classic Cartland cad. He was one of the first men to scale Mont Blanc and he claimed to have slept with women of every nationality in the world, voting Japanese 'much the best'. Educated at Winchester and Trinity, Oxford, he was a retired colonel with a vile temper, but also, incontestably, a Victorian country gent with attitudes to match.

As such he regarded Grandfather Cartland with snobbish hostility. 'You're selling yourself on the altar for seven and six,' he used to say to his daughter Polly, once she became engaged to Bertie Cartland. As Dame Barbara records, 'Colonel Scobell disliked the thought of his daughter having anything to do with business.'

Polly and Bertie met at the High Sheriff's Ball in Worcester in 1897. Polly had gone there with her rich and glamorous friends the Greswolde Williamses. Polly was enjoying a waltz when Bertie, 'six foot tall, good-looking, with light-blue eyes which always seemed to have a twinkle in them', entered the room and apparently said to himself, 'That is the girl I am going to marry.'

Unfortunately, and one feels uncharacteristically, Bertie was a non-dancer. Later he used to become enraged with jealousy when he saw Polly dancing with another man and now, at the Sheriff's Ball, he was unable to sweep his intended off her pretty little feet as he would have done in a Cartland novel. He hunted five days a week, raced under his own colours, played polo and cricket, was a crack shot, but he did not declare his love until March 1899 at the Adelphi Hotel in Liverpool where the ubiquitous Greswolde Williamses had got up a party for the Grand National. Bertie proposed on a sofa in a corridor outside Polly's bedroom and was turned down. 'Absolutely could not say yes,' Polly confided to her diary. Bertie, not used to having no for an answer, nevertheless wrote to Polly saying, 'That I was ass enough to hope that you might be something to me is entirely my own fault.'

But Bertie persevered and a year later, after a show (*Floradora*) and supper at the Savoy, he proposed again in Frank Greswolde Williams's room at Brown's Hotel. This time Polly said yes.

Colonel Scobell was not amused.

There were fearful rows over the marriage settlement. Polly's diary for June 1900 is full of them: 'Father in a very bad temper' on the 23rd. 'Row. Father beastly' on the 24th. 'Worse rows. Father like a mad man,' on the 25th. And so on until 30 June when: 'Rows better . . . Father rather nicer . . . cried less.' All attempts to arrive at a mutually agreed settlement had been called off. On 5 July the pair were married at St Bartholomew's Church, Redmarley and on the drive to the church her father the Colonel kept repeating that she was selling herself on the altar for seven and six and would never be happy. He wept as he kissed her goodbye but at the end of the drive the bride turned to Bertie and exclaimed, 'What a relief! To think this is the end of the rows!'

For Polly this was 'a ripping year'. Her father-in-law bought them a house near Pershore and paid off Bertie's debts which amounted to nine hundred pounds. He also offered him two thousand pounds a year thereafter, plus a hundred pounds every Christmas and birthday. In addition he paid for two gardeners and the young couple themselves employed a couple of grooms while Polly had a lady's maid, a parlourmaid, a housemaid and a cook – each of whom was paid about twenty pounds a year. Life seems to have been nothing but tea and tennis in summer, hunting, shooting and balls in winter.

In July 1901 the heroine of this story arrived in the manner already described but nothing very much seemed to change in this happy household. Life continued to be more or less ripping until disaster struck on Sunday 16 October 1903.

James Cartland's affairs had prospered and the Master of Vectis Lodge appeared to be a rich and successful man. However, he overstepped himself in the matter of the Fishguard railway, rather curiously described by Dame Barbara as 'the shortest route to Holyhead'. Then, as now, the sea-crossing from Fishguard to Rosslare was the shortest between Great Britain and Ireland and a railway between London and the South Wales port was an eminently sensible idea. So Mr Cartland thought and he accordingly borrowed a quarter of a million pounds from the bank in order to invest in it. Alas there was a slump and the banks, as is their wont, called in their cash.

Mr Cartland might have survived this crisis, given some financial legerdemain and belt tightening, but he lacked support from his wife – Dame Barbara has revealed that 'he had a discreet little friend round the corner' – and he simply was not up to the challenge. That Sunday morning he went out and shot himself dead.

This was obviously a financial as well as a personal tragedy for the young Cartlands. Because of those fearful rows between their fathers the marriage settlement had never been officially signed and sealed. The beautiful house near Pershore was therefore part of the deceased's estate. So was the furniture. And, of course, there was no way that the generous allowances and the paying of servants could continue. All that was left was the two hundred pounds a year from Mrs Cartland and a grudging hundred pounds from the Colonel to his daughter. In the end they were allowed to keep the furniture – but only on loan. It could be repossessed at any moment.

Polly, more energetic and resourceful than her husband, went house-hunting and discovered an acceptable old farmhouse in Pershore called Amerie Court. It belonged to the Earl of Coventry and he was prepared to let them have it for forty pounds a year. It had eight bedrooms and a tennis court but the water had to be pumped and there was an old kitchen range in the dining-room which they could not afford to move. Nevertheless they kept one of their horses and took on a nurse and a general maid at eighteen and ten pounds a year respectively. Polly had to polish the remaining silver herself. Bertie, meanwhile, pottered in the garden, drank heavily and resisted his mother's and father-in-law's admonitions to get himself a job. After all, he had never been trained for one. Besides he was not well. The drinking brought on what Dame Barbara, in one of her memoirs, describes as 'heart attacks' though there were so many that they would surely have killed him had they been as severe as the description sounds.

Nevertheless they kept up appearances as best they could, despite having to bicycle to many of their social engagements. They bicycled to hounds, they bicycled to tennis and they bicycled to shooting. If it was too far to cycle they took the train. When Mrs Cartland died a little later – the tightness of her corsets apparently inducing a cancer – their income leaped up by three hundred pounds a year. This welcome bonus still didn't pay off the debts and Bertie, unfortunately, tried to solve the problem by gambling. On a spectacular day at Birmingham Races he lost three hundred pounds. Polly sold her turquoise-and-diamond necklace and Bertie pawned his guns, but still the writs flowed in.

Despairing, Polly approached her father, the irascible Colonel, but predictably he flew into a rage on discovering his son-in-law's betting accounts and threatened to cut them off altogether unless the wretched Bertie got a job. They then approached Bertie's uncle George, a barrister turned industrialist. Uncle George proved a softer touch than the Colonel. He paid off the debts and took control of their finances, allowing them just enough for housekeeping until everything was on a more or less even keel.

Bertie's first move towards what one might call a job came about a year after the birth of their second child christened John Ronald Hamilton but known throughout his all too brief life as Ronald. Ronald was later to make his reputation in politics as a Conservative MP and it was the Conservative party which changed the life of his father in 1909. The catalyst was their local parliamentary candidate, a retired naval officer called Bolton Eyres-Monsell. Polly and Bertie heard him speak and were so impressed that they subsequently joined the Primrose League. This organisation, named after Benjamin Disraeli's favourite flower, was the nearest the party had to an organisation. It had about two million members divided up into two thousand area 'Habitations'. As his daughter Dame Barbara recalls blithely, 'He had, of course, been a Conservative all his life, but he hadn't thought much about politics before.' Within a fortnight of his joining the League Captain Bertram Cartland had become the Honorary Secretary of the newly formed Pershore 'Habitation'.

The job was unpaid but nevertheless it was more of a job than gardening and Bertie seems to have been quite a success. Before long he was appointed Secretary of the County Council of the League and was being described in the local press as 'hard working' and 'thoroughly acquainted with the(ir) work'. The promotion was only slightly marred by his being fined five shillings with four shillings costs for riding his bicycle on a footpath.

During the 1910 General Election Bertie acted as agent for Eyres-Monsell with such success that he asked him to become his political secretary at a salary of a hundred and fifty pounds a year. The Eyres-Monsells also asked the Cartlands on holiday to Switzerland where Stanley Baldwin, another Worcestershire MP, was staying in the same hotel, together with his cousin Rudyard Kipling. Bertie apparently struck up an acquaintance with Kipling who was pleased to learn that the eight-year-old Barbara had recently learned 'with some difficulty' his poem, 'Where are you going to, all you big Steamers?' Polly, for her part, 'became firm friends with Stanley Baldwin' on the nursery slopes where they were both learning to ski.

Her parents had never quite forgiven little Barbara for being a girl (a recurring family trait) and Ronald's arrival made her jealous. Soon after he was born she asked her mother to send the new baby back where he had come from on the grounds that 'everyone asks after him and no one asks after me'. Ronald was a precocious politician, making speeches in the nursery when he was only three years old. Barbara, by contrast, was considered rather dull and on the plain side especially after losing her milk teeth. Her best features were thought to be her shapely legs and feet, though this only caused her mother's friends to remark that if she continued to be as plain when she 'came out' she would have to be made to walk on her head. Despite this she professes to have been devoted to her brother, almost from the very first.

In 1911 Bertie secured another hundred pounds a year, plus expenses, when he was made Provincial Secretary of the Primrose League for the whole of Worcestershire, Warwickshire, Herefordshire, Shropshire and Gloucestershire.

Colonel Scobell died the following year from a heart attack brought on by one of his ungovernable rages. An outhouse near the pigsties caught fire and the Colonel was furious with the Tewkesbury fire brigade for not getting there in time to save it. This was Barbara's first bereavement and she 'wept because she knew it was the right thing to do'. Ronald's response was equally characteristic. Their mother had a rug in her bedroom made up from the remains of a favourite shaggy-haired terrier called Rags. What Ronald wanted to know was: 'Will Grandpa be made into a rug like Rags?'

Barbara's first school was Worcester High where she went in the company of the Cavendish-Bentinck girls, Berry and Alice. The Cavendish-Bentincks provided a dog-cart to the local railway station and a governess to escort them to and from school. Barbara did the final leg home on the back of her father's or a neighbour's bike. When the Cavendish-Bentincks moved from their idyllic home at Burlington House ('which I loved') she was sent to Malvern which she hated. The girls thought her 'uppish'. She thought them noisy and rather common. This mutual antipathy between Barbara and the rest of her sex was to continue throughout her life.

In 1914 she became a boarder. The family moved from Worcestershire to a London flat because Bertie had a new job, planning the evacuation of ten thousand women and children from Ulster. Large quantities of arms had been shipped into the province from Germany and civil unrest was expected. The job of getting women and children to the mainland was entrusted to the Primrose League who in turn entrusted it to Bertie. In his time off he managed to take Barbara to a show called *Hello Ragtime* at the Hippodrome. Barbara remembers the chorus girls with 'their well-accentuated figures with pronounced bosoms and curved hips beneath small, nipped-in waists' and the crowds of Stage Door Johnnies waiting for them in top hats. It is already a recognisably Barbara Cartland image.

Later that year the family returned to Amerie Court and Bertie was called up. He and Polly enjoyed a romantic interlude while he was in training – 'she sat in his tent and mended his clothes' – at a camp near Plymouth and later at Broadlands in Hampshire, home of a new friend, the immensely wealthy Wilfred Ashley whose daughter Edwina was later to marry Lord Mountbatten. Then on 4 November, from a hotel room in Southampton, she watched him march past with his regiment, bound for France and the front. 'He looked up and waved,' according to Barbara. 'She managed to smile at him, but after that she could see nothing for tears.'

Barbara remembers no special goodbye of her own. Indeed she remembers that at that time he wanted more than anything to be alone 'with Mummy'. Despite the bucking-up effect of Ronald's birth, after which he had not only got a job but also given up alcohol, Bertie does not sound a particularly doting father.

As soon as Bertie had gone to the war, Polly shut up Amerie Court and went to live with her mother, the Widow Scobell. Barbara was taken away from school at Malvern and sent to families, first in Bath and then to Nailsea Court nearby. In Bath she shared a governess with an older girl of 'suitable' family who bullied her. She was miserable and also much influenced by religion. Polly was a strong Anglo-Catholic and Barbara used to say evening prayers in her bedroom with a crucifix and lighted candles. It was at this time that she had her first mystical experience. An angel appeared to her during prayers one evening in Bath. At Nailsea, in the bosom of the family of a widower, Commander Evans, she was happier but experienced ghosts. She remains susceptible to such things. When she heard the ghost of a stricken civil war Cavalier coming upstairs she repeated the prayer her mother had taught her: 'Lighten our darkness we beseech Thee O Lord, and by thy great mercy defend us from all perils and dangers of the night.' Over sixty years later she said that 'to this day whenever I am in a house haunted by some tormented soul I always repeat it'.

She was growing up fast and turning into an attractive young woman, leggy, blonde and with luminous green eyes later known to her admirers as 'Barbara's headlights'. They clearly captivated one house guest, a romantically inclined major who invited Barbara to his bedroom to 'show her how his revolver worked'. Barbara, being young, fell for this unlikely story, partly, she later said, because the major's bedroom was next door to the Billiard Room. 'Had he asked me to his bedroom upstairs,' she said, 'naturally I wouldn't have gone.' The major duly demonstrated his revolver, emptying the chamber and then, to demonstrate that he had done so, pointed the weapon at Barbara and with the words, 'Now it's empty,' pulled the trigger and watched with horror as a live round whizzed passed Barbara's temple. She says she was deaf for forty-eight hours and that she had 'never seen a man go so green'.

She was isolated from her family throughout the war years and felt the isolation painfully. She wrote regularly to Bertie but it was Polly, 'the sweetest, dearest, prettiest, angelest, rippingest, adorable Mother anyone ever had', whom she missed most of all. 'I do love to have you all to myself,' she wrote, 'without any of the family wanting you too.'

The Nailsea Court sojourn came to an end after two years and Barbara was sent to a finishing school on the Solent called Netley Abbey. This she enjoyed. The headmistress was agreeably progressive and even mentioned divorce one day – a revelation that Barbara, in a letter home, highlighted with three exclamation marks. Even in extreme old age she remained addicted to superlative punctuation and 'screamers', particularly in private correspondence.

She also continued to have curious psychic experiences. On one occasion, after illicitly finding a copy of the previous day's casualty list and becoming depressed by the long list of deaths, she went back to her room and found it full of the smell of fresh violets. It was not the only time in her life when distant death was manifested by the smell of flowers impossible to explain.

And then, in 1917, her mother was having tea with Mrs Scobell one hot day in May when the butler came in with one of those telegrams from the War Office. It regretted that Major J.B.F. Cartland of the Worcester Regiment had been killed in action. The Army Council expressed sympathy. He was forty-one years old.

The teenage Barbara did not weep for her father, as she had wept for Grandfather Scobell, but she did the right thing. 'My Ownest Darling,' she wrote to her mother, 'I can't tell you how I loved your letter. I think you are simply *too* wonderful. No wonder Daddy loved you as he did – and does.'

The letter is full of love for Polly, pride in father, oddly lacking in any overt display of grief, even to the extent of saying, 'In a way, it's lovely to remember him so young and cheery.'

It is signed 'Babs' and underneath there is a footnote of precocious, almost chilling practicality: 'I have had my coat and skirt dyed black. Would you like me to have my coat-frock done?'

34

Chapter Three

Barbara 'comes out'. Men find her very attrac-
tive. She is thrilled. But she has no money so
she becomes a journalist. She is spotted by
Lord Beaverbrook. He also finds Barbara
very attractive. She becomes a novelist.

I t was a year after her father's
death that, at Bembridge on the Isle of Wight, she first found
out about men. Hitherto the men in her life had been her
two younger brothers, her father and her grandfather. There
might have been the odd exception like the libidinous major
with the revolver but generally speaking she had led a sexually cloistered and innocent life unimaginable today. Although
she was eighteen years old she had been treated, like other
members of her generation, class and sex, as little more than
a child.

Now, however, she was 'coming out' and, suddenly, she
was not only exposed to men, she was expected to be 'amusing, gay and attractive'. And to her unconcealed delight, she
was. Although, on her own admission, she was only a pale
imitation of every man's dream girl, Gladys Cooper, she was
still in the same mould: 'Fair hair fluffed over the ears, large
rather surprised eyes – mine were actually green – red lips,
subject of much criticism and many arguments, and a clear
skin helped by a chalk-white face powder.' She says she was
also 'incredibly ignorant' which was probably no handicap.

Polly, desolate and – by the standards to which she

aspired – destitute, had taken a holiday house there because she had been told that it was 'a gay and amusing place for the young'. Barbara had left the finishing school in July 1919 and now, here she was, unleashed on an unspecting Isle of Wight.

One night on the beach a man told her that he was unable to live without her and wished to marry her. Barbara was thrilled. 'This was living! This was life! This was being alone with a man!' What made the occasion even more remarkable was that evidently it was the third such proposal in a fortnight. She was in danger of becoming blasé. Not that the proposals were uniformly flattering. The first was from a forty-year-old colonel with a red moustache.

In her first year of independence Barbara had an allowance of fifty pounds. The family were very poor but under Polly's indomitable leadership they were damned if they would let it show. Barbara once said that something her mother had done was 'common' whereupon little Polly flared up and declared, 'Poor I may be but common I am not.' The remark was adopted, only half humorously, as the family motto. Polly also once rounded on her children when she detected a lack of gratitude and said, 'I work my fingers to the bone – and not a word of thanks.' 'Not a word of thanks' also became part of the family lexicon.

Throughout the war they had lived in rented accommodation around Tewkesbury, where in the Abbey, Polly commissioned a memorial tablet to Bertie. You can find it just inside the gates. Tewkesbury, however, was not Barbara's idea of fun, particularly after the excitement of the Isle of Wight and when Polly asked her where she wanted to live Barbara, who had only ever been there once in her life, just before the war when Bertie took her to the theatre, immediately opted for London. Polly, who didn't care where she lived, provided she was with her daughter and – during school holidays – her sons, acquiesced and, through friends, managed to rent a 'tall, dingy house', Number 20 Neville Road, in South Kensington, just off the Fulham Road by the Brompton Hospital. It had once been a fashionable part of town but was not considered so in 1919.

On their first evening there Barbara and Ronald took a stroll and ended up in what seemed to them the rather intimidating hubbub outside South Kensington tube station. This was one of those moments that Dame Barbara looks back on as a landmark. Suddenly overawed by life, by London, and particularly by their mother's daunting expectations of them, they clutched each other's hands and made solemn promises.

'I', said Barbara, 'shall get to know everybody – everybody in London.'

Ronald said, solemnly, that he, for his part, was going to be Prime Minister.

At first it looked as if the latter ambition was the more plausible. They may have been in the very swim of pre-war Worcester society but in London they knew practically nobody. In despair Barbara took to going to the *thé-dansants* given every Sunday by Maud Kerr-Smiley.

Polly, who disapproved of fun on the Sabbath, clearly had problems in reconciling her religious beliefs with her social ambitions for her daughter. A way out was soon found. Barbara was to teach at the St Paul's, Knightsbridge Sunday School in the mornings. Her approach to this task was unorthodox. Nobody told her what she should teach the children, nor were her lessons supervised. 'I told them dramatic stories,' she recalled, 'inventing them as I went along and serialising them, so we started where we left off the previous Sunday.' Feeling virtuous she would then go off to the 'Church Parade' in Hyde Park. This was a sort of High Society '*paseo*' involving one lot of people sitting on green chairs in Stanhope Gardens while another lot of people drove or walked past. Here Barbara would hope to pick up a young man who would take her to lunch at Claridge's. And so on to Mrs Kerr-Smiley's *thé-dansant*.

Mrs Kerr-Smiley was the sister of Ernest Simpson who was later to achieve a sort of second-hand notoriety as the husband of Wallis. Barbara danced often with Ernest at the big house in Belgrave Square but was warned by his sister that he was going to have to marry money. On one occasion Ernest tried to kiss her in the back of a taxi. Barbara was having none of it. She was strongly averse to being 'mauled'. Kissing could wait until she was safely married.

As far as men were concerned she seems to have carried on, once she had effected a few introductions, much as she had done on the Isle of Wight. Several suitors followed in the footsteps of the colonel with the red moustache and eventually she accepted a young Irish officer in the Life Guards called Dick Usher. Having taken this important decision she thought it prudent to ask her mother to tell her how babies were made. She was so 'shocked and horrified' by what she was told that she broke off the engagement.

Dick, presumably neither shocked nor horrified by the baby-making process, took this badly. So badly that he threatened to shoot himself outside the coffee stall in Hyde Park where debs and their delights habitually went for a late-night drink and a clandestine cuddle. Barbara, remembering the trigger-happy major of a few years earlier, was disposed to take him seriously, but it was thirteen years before Dick really did shoot himself. He crashed his plane in Africa while on honeymoon, killing his bride. He evidently survived but when rescuers arrived they found his body with a revolver in his hand and a note saying 'I have killed my darling and I no longer wish to live'.

The romantic novelist had plenty of real life from which to draw. Years later, in the drawing-room at Camfield Place, the ninety-two-year-old Dame Barbara looked back wonderingly on an era when sex was simply not discussed, when 'Will you marry me?' was the contemporary equivalent of 'Your place or mine?' and when a negative reply was frequently met with a threat to shoot oneself. Young men who had survived the Somme still kept their service revolvers and they had seen so much carnage that they were not unduly concerned about their own mortality.

Everyone in her set during the twenties was intensely romantic. Or so she says. Her explanation for this is that 'marriage was considered indissoluble. Marriage was the goal, the prize, the grand finale of our hopes and aspirations. There was no continuation of the story because there was no question of there ever being a divorce later.' She says that in 1914 divorce cases were only a quarter of one per cent of all law cases that came to court. It simply didn't happen.

Perhaps this was part of the reason. In the 1990s the old Barbara Cartland found it increasingly frustrating to try to explain the thoughts and behaviour of her generation. Everything had changed so totally that it was, she used to say, hopeless even trying to explain.

In any event, *We Danced All Night* seems to have been a fair title for her own 'dazzling portrait of a glittering era'. When, as a very old woman, she wrote a treatment for a film of her life called, 'I Follow My Secret Heart', she wanted 'flashes of Barbara dancing at three or four different places'. The first of these, she thought, should be, 'The Grafton Galleries where the young people danced in the Exhibition Room to a Black Band. If the pictures are at all nude they are covered over at night with a piece of tissue paper, but this may be difficult to explain. The men are all wearing white tie and tails and the girls pretty evening dresses, not too *decolletée*.

'In the last flash you see them twirling round, which has just come in, with the tails of the men's coats swinging out as they twirl and twirl around the room. MUSIC: "Ain't We Got Fun" and "Let's do it".'

That was part of her story of the twenties and perhaps for some of the bright young things it really was. In most societies there are those who have the time, money and inclination to lead a life devoted entirely to self-indulgence and these people invariably seem to attract a disproportionate amount of publicity. Barbara, however, was not like that. To be sure she twirled and twirled, and danced and dazzled and had fun, fun, fun but, in truth, she had neither the time, money nor inclination to do just that. Her family was – relatively – poor; she was intensely ambitious even if that ambition was unfocused. The combination of this fierce determination and the need to earn money meant that there simply wasn't time for 'all play'.

Yet she had no qualifications for earning money. Nor indeed, as she was later to admit, *any* serious qualifications. All she had been taught was how to make herself attractive to men and that was very nearly it. It is impossible now to be sure about the matter of her attractiveness. Photographs of her in her twenties portray a wholesome but frankly quite ordinary appearance. In her first volume of autobiography she reproduces a picture of herself alongside seven contemporaries. To the right are four 'Exquisites', whose style, glamour and beauty is still obvious after all these years. They are Lady Plunket, Anne Messel (mother of the present Lord Snowdon), The Prince of Wales's friend Mrs Dudley Ward and Sylvia Hawkes who went on to have five husbands. She puts herself among the 'Bright Young People', the others being Loelia Ponsonby (later Westminster) and Daphne Vivien (later Weymouth) both of whom look more beautiful and Eleanor Smith who looks a lot funnier. Barbara, in a 'Crusader' cloche hat, three strings of pearls and what looks like some sort of fur, looks quite plain, even –

and this will astonish those who, like me, only know the much later extraordinary vision in pink – quite ordinary. She does, however, wear an expression of cool and intelligent appraisal which a forensic examiner might consider potentially dangerous. She does not look as if she is going to suffer fools.

The fact remains that she certainly had not been taught how to earn a living. She had, as the Sunday School experience had demonstrated, an innate ability to tell stories, and she had a perfectly adequate – if somewhat breathless – command of written English. Nowadays that would send her straight into the arms of the Peterborough Column of the *Daily Telegraph* or the *Evening Standard*'s Londoner's Diary. Or to a trendy literary agent. But in those days life was not like that.

Instead she met a man at a cocktail party one evening and he turned out to work for the *Daily Express*. He said that if Barbara cared to send him snippets for the gossip column he would pay her five shillings for each paragraph published. He was the Dempster of the day. This seemed an extraordinarily easy way of making money and she proved successful at it. After the five-shilling paragraphs for the diary she swiftly moved on to feature articles which paid in guineas. This was serious money. 'Miss Cartland,' said the blurb above her first *Express* feature, 'who is twenty-two, exemplifies in London Society, the charming and intellectually exuberant type she describes.' From the very first her articles were intensely personal and highly opinionated, as they have remained throughout her life. Her worst enemy would never accuse her of being objective! Thus, in her first article, defending herself and her generation she wrote that 'Youth acting on an impulse, fired with the spirit of an idea, disregarding the consequences, demanding the compliance of its desires in an instant, and forging ahead to attain them –

43

who shall condemn it?' As Henry Cloud remarked, 'Certainly not the *Express*.' The paper gave her full rein and before long the young writer was expressing opinions that she was to continue articulating for seventy years and more – the weakness of men, (despite their 'wonderfulness'), the perils of drink, the duties of women. And so on. These effusions were popular. So much so that after a few weeks the phone went and she was told that Lord Beaverbrook wished to meet her.

Beaverbrook, 'the Gnome of New Brunswick', was already forty-four years old and one of the great adventurers of the times. He was then, in 1923, in the early stages of turning the *Sunday* and *Daily Express* and the *Evening Standard* newspapers into the most successful and charismatic papers in Britain. Although he did so by delegating to brilliant editors, most notably Arthur Christiansen at the *Daily Express*, he was a hands-on proprietor in a sense not easily understood nowadays. Beaverbrook adored making mischief, he enjoyed the company of journalists, and above all he got a real frisson of excitement from spotting and nurturing young talent, especially female. Even in his eighties he was still firing off notes and making phone calls in those inimitable rasping tones to bright female graduate trainees sixty years his junior.

It was no surprise, therefore, that he should spot the young Barbara Cartland. She had just the well-connected *jeu d'esprit* which attracted him. It also appealed to his three great cronies – F.E. Smith (Lord Birkenhead), Winston Churchill and Sir James Dunn. Young Barbara thought of them as 'The Four Adventurers'. She became a regular lunch and dinner guest at Beaverbrook's house in Hurlingham, the Vineyards. 'I suppose', she later mused, 'I was a perfect audience because I was prepared to listen wide-eyed, and maybe open-mouthed, to everything they told me. I was also so young and so ignorant that they could repeat old stories, old anecdotes, and know that to me they were as new and fresh as on the day when they first happened.

'I think that in a way these great men enjoyed showing off to a young girl. They certainly talked to me, and perhaps at that particular time they needed someone to talk to.'

The sadness, in a sense, is that she was too young and naive fully to appreciate them. 'In those days', she recalled later, 'older men were not people. I couldn't believe that they suffered, that they were ever unhappy, depressed or despondent as I and my contemporaries often were. I couldn't believe that they felt deeply about anything except finance and success, which we had not yet tasted. They were creatures apart, made of granite or gold, but not of fears and tears, of shyness and half-formed aspirations which we felt would never come true.' Not that she was all *that* overawed. Her first reaction on meeting him was that he was just like a good-luck charm she had carried in the war. It was called 'Billikens'.

Whatever she really felt at the time it must have been an extraordinary experience for a young woman in her early twenties who did not have the advantage of coming from one of the great aristocratic or political families of Britain. True, Beaverbrook and his friends would have enjoyed the open-mouthed, wide-eyed adulation of such a young woman, but if that was all they were after there were plenty of other young women of more beauty and better breeding. They must have recognised a particular quality in her which was lacking in her rivals – a mixture of more obvious beauty and aristocratic background. The young Barbara had 'something' but it was a something so elusive that those who attempted to define it ultimately gave up and called it 'it'. Whatever it was she had it.

'Max taught me to write,' she says. 'I believe it is entirely due to him that I have been so successful with my books and the thousands of articles I have done over the years.'

45

On that very first visit to the Vineyard he told her that she wrote well but could write better. Then he bombarded her with questions about who she was, where she came from, why she wrote and what she thought. Thereafter she would take her *Express* and *Standard* paragraphs to the Hyde Park Hotel where Beaverbrook maintained a phone-filled office. There he would make a great performance of cross-questioning her about what she had written, then pulling her article into little pieces and crossing out the superfluities until finally he applied the proprietorial initials of approval and the authorised version went off to the paper for automatic inclusion.

The trouble, of course, was that Beaverbrook's idea of how to write was highly individual. He liked opinions expressed with certainty in short paragraphs, short sentences and short words. This was a fine formula for popular newspapers but not, alas, for great literature. The Beaver's influence is easily detected in Barbara Cartland's romantic fiction and I am not at all convinced that the influence is wholly benign. It was he, for instance, who told her to include as many names as possible, particularly if they were aristocratic. This might have been sound advice for the William Hickey column or Jennifer's Diary. For a novelist, even one who specialises in romantic historicals, it can be dangerous. Fiction which reads like a narrative version of *Debrett's* can seem, especially at this end of the twentieth century, unfashionable to say the least.

On one of her visits to the Hyde Park Hotel Lord Beaverbrook asked her to kiss him. Or so Dame Barbara used to say. From what one knows of Beaverbrook it seems more likely that he would have helped himself without asking and I rather assume that 'asking for a kiss' is a euphemism for asking her to go to bed with him. In her autobiographical film treatment, 'I Follow My Secret Heart', Dame Barbara suggests that the scene takes place immediately after she has declined an offer of marriage from Sir James Dunn. In this version Beaverbrook says (slowly and quietly), 'I cannot offer you marriage. But if you love me, I could make you the most famous journalist in the world.' To which she replies, 'No! No! Of course not! And now I must go home.' In his book Henry Cloud unequivocally states that Beaverbrook wanted to make her his mistress. In any event Barbara declined the offer and relations between the two were never again quite the same.

The Hyde Park Hotel seems to have had a notably aphrodisiac effect on men in the twenties. On another occasion Michael Arlen, author of *The Green Hat*, invited her to his room in the hotel. When she got there she found Arlen in bed where he invited her to join him. Barbara said she'd absolutely love to but unfortunately she had another appointment. Whereupon she fled. Her mother, Polly, had warned her that she must always decline men's proposals with the greatest possible tact in order not to hurt their feelings. All her life she has remembered this basic maternal rule.

Her career as a novelist just pre-dated her first encounter with the Canadian tycoon, albeit tentatively. She started writing *Jigsaw* before meeting him, but it was not published until 1923, by which time she was well embarked on those early Beaverbrook tutorials at the Hyde Park.

It was during the school holidays when her beloved Ronald was at home from Charterhouse and revising for exams. A bored Barbara took one of his notebooks and started to scribble what was in effect a highly romanticised autobiography, a sort of first person 'if-only'. Her son Ian maintains that all his mother's novels are variations on the Cinderella theme and certainly this début, as everyone, including Barbara, concedes, is recognisably Cinderella. It has to be said, however, that in later years Dame Barbara barely acknowledged this first novel.

The book was sent to Duckworth on spec and published on the same day that the firm also published Edith Sitwell's *Troy Park*. A strange pair of bedfellows indeed. *Jigsaw* cost seven shillings and six pence and attracted publicity outside the book pages because the author was a young society lady and such people were not expected to write books of any kind, let alone mildly sexy novels taking the lid off the world in which they moved. The reviews themselves were 'mixed'. One, for example, thought it 'vivid and moving . . . a dramatic conflict of emotions, written with zest and freshness which will win the admiration of all readers'. Another said she must either be 'very inexperienced' or 'an extraordinarily guileless woman' and thought the book 'simply a mix of the old-fashioned novelette and the modern feverish novel of the amateur'.

Win some, lose some. On its own *Jigsaw* was not going to make Barbara Cartland rich or famous. But it was a beginning. And she was still only twenty-three.

Chapter Four

Everyone has a gay time at the Embassy
Club. Barbara tells me about some of her
'affaires'. She decides it is time to settle down.
She marries.

'On Thursday nights', according to the young Barbara Cartland, 'everyone went to the Embassy Club.' These were the twenties and for the privileged few it was party time. 'Everyone' was anyone who was anyone. The club was at the Piccadilly end of Bond Street and there were bouncers on the door. Michael Arlen said of these men that they were the 'best shifters of their kind'. Their job, like that of their successors today who admit the genuine glitterati while excluding the ordinary punters from whatever happens to be the Embassy of the moment, was to 'sift out the low and vulgar from the fashionable'.

There was a song to celebrate the Embassy's Thursday nights, just as there seemed to be sardonic Cowardish songs to celebrate practically everything in the twenties.

> *There's the famous and notorious*
> *There's the rich and there's the poor,*
> *There's film-stars, Peers and Peeresses,*
> *All crowded on the floor.*
> *There's the Prince of Wales and Lady F.*
> *And who else do I see?*
> *But every crashing bore I know*
> *In the dear old Embassy!*

My dear, everyone was there. At the entrance, at the end of a long, low tunnel, you bought a gardenia or a carnation from a small one-legged man, the warmth of whose effusions were a signal of your status. Once inside, you would hope to exchange a word with Lady Diana Cooper and then if you were really grand you would park yourself on one of the sofas around the walls. Less grand and you would have to make do with a table by the minute parquet dance floor which grew smaller and smaller as the night wore on and the crowd increased. 'It was', said Barbara, 'the smartest place in the whole of Europe.'

Alas, by the 1990s most of this smart set had passed on to the great dance floor in the sky and it was difficult to see precisely how Barbara Cartland fitted in with it. Most of the witnesses were no longer around to be cross-examined. Nevertheless there are one or two interesting verdicts. One acquaintance of Barbara's recalled a catty verdict from a mutual friend. 'There were the Belgravia dances,' she said, 'and there were the Pont Street ones. I'm afraid Barbara was definitely Pont Street.' Such social nuances mean nothing today but in the twenties they spoke volumes.

Betty Kenward, for instance, who later became the doyenne of gossip columnists as 'Jennifer' of Jennifer's Diary, was five years her junior but got to know her through her brothers who were at Charterhouse with Ronald.

'Barbara', she recalled later, 'seemed absolutely fabulous to me in those days! She used to tell me some of the romantic episodes going on in her life, usually involving a duke, or at least an earl! Her imagination used to carry her away and I lapped up every word she spoke. I have often since then wondered if I was a sort of trial run for the secretaries to whom she dictates her vastly successful novels from a *chaise-longue* each afternoon.'

Dame Barbara was rather frosty about Mrs Kenward in later life. She seemed to think Jennifer didn't like her, despite the fact that Barbara gave her her first break on the *Tatler*. Perhaps that has something to do with it. Nevertheless the picture of Barbara in the twenties as a genuine exotic with a tendency to artistic licence is both interesting and plausible.

Oddly enough I had just written that paragraph when Dame Barbara telephoned from Scotland and said that on the way up she and Ian had stayed with friends where Mrs Kenward was staying. 'I cut her,' she said. She didn't speak to her at dinner and didn't say goodbye to her the following morning. Mrs Kenward was evidently upset by this but the feud is long-standing and deep. The Dame can be implacable in her dislikes. Mrs Kenward's crime had been to make a slighting reference to her connections with the Royal Family. I mentioned that I was going to quote her in this book. 'Oh don't put her in,' she said. 'Don't give her the satisfaction.'

As so often with such ephemeral sensations, the success of the Embassy was down to one individual, a man known as Luigi who appears to have been a cross between Mark Birley, Stringfellow and the late Peter Langan. He knew everyone, he knew everyone's secrets, and he could apparently 'dress' a room better than anyone else, arranging his clientele with the ultimate social precision.

And then Luigi died and the Prince of Wales and Lady F. and Lady Diana and even the crashing bores all drifted away. The proprietors, in a panic, spent a fortune on a disastrous refurbishment but still the Embassy languished. Without Luigi it was simply an ugly room at the end of a tunnel at the Piccadilly end of Bond Street.

They needed a new Luigi and in their wisdom they sent for Barbara. Barbara made them change the décor to match her own signature colours of pink and greeny-blue which she had become enchanted with during a visit to the Pharaohs' tombs in 1927. They became the colours of her boudoir, they are still the prevailing colours at Camfield Place from the park gates on, they are the colours she likes in her clothes and her make-up and they helped to magnetise that elusive 'everyone' back to the Embassy after she had taken over.

In *We Danced All Night* she spends some thirty pages describing a Thursday night at the Embassy. It's really something of a *tour de force*, not least because she plays faster and looser than usual with Beaverbrook's advice on how to write English. There is even a ten-line paragraph and a thirty-seven-word sentence. However, she does remember the Beaver's dictum about the dropping of names. There is Lady Plunket, floating in the arms of Prince George; the Vicomtesse de Janze (great-granddaughter of Mrs Jordan and William IV), Mrs Wilfred Ashley (with the biggest green ostrich-feather fan in the house), the Countess of Portarlington, the first woman to decorate her drawing-room in pale oyster; her husband the Earl, 'that damned cuckoo' who arrives independently and spends all his time chatting up other women; Alec and Mary Cunningham-Reid in a large party including Charlie Chaplin; Edwina and Dickie Mountbatten; Lady Diana Cooper; the Morgan sisters – Thelma Furness and Gloria Vanderbilt; various Cadogan sisters, known collectively as 'the Pack'; a dark horse called 'the Borstal Boy' – 'All women love a devil and all women imagine they can reform one'; Prince Aly Khan, the supreme sexual technician who – a story Barbara much enjoys telling in later years – is supposed to have maintained three mistresses simultaneously on separate floors of the Ritz Hotel, keeping them all in a state of supreme sexual satisfaction and ignorance of each other; Lord Molyneux; Burghie, Earl of Westmorland; Cecil Beaton who 'has become the rage'; Michael Arlen who has arrived in a yellow Rolls Royce; Sir John ('Buffles') and

Lady Milbanke; the Hon. Mrs Richard Norton ('recently tried her hand at running a cinema') and her husband, later Lord Grantley ('slightly hunch-backed, looks like Richard III'); Lord Brownlow; Paula Gellibrand; Lionel Tennyson, the cricketer and his wife Clare, Lord Glenconner's sister; Lady Alexandra Metcalfe and her husband 'Fruity'; The Prince of Wales and Freda Dudley Ward; and finally the club cat, Embassy Jackson, black as your hat and given to stalking along the backs of the sofas bringing good luck to the clientele.

Thus, 'Everyone' on Thursday night at the Embassy. And thus the scene that the young Barbara was hired to recreate after the death of Maître Luigi. She succeeded, apparently all too well. All too well because she was hired on a commission basis and once the club was back on the rails it dispensed with her services.

The point is not so much that she made a bad deal but that unlike nearly all her society friends she was in a position where she was compelled to make deals in order to survive. The Cartlands had no private means and somehow wealth had to be created. *Jigsaw* and its successors were not written because Barbara had a burning literary ambition but because she needed the cash. Her mother Polly briefly ran a woollens shop called Knitwear in Sloane Street but the strain made her seriously ill. Afterwards Barbara herself ran a shop. Hers sold hats but it didn't last because, as she herself admits, whenever a potential customer called the proprietor was invariably out to lunch – usually wearing one of the best hats herself.

The obvious way out of this financial fix was marriage and on her own evidence there was no shortage of suitors. Her estimate, universally accepted, is that about fifty men proposed marriage to her before she finally accepted. The figure is impossible to contest, yet it presumably includes those callow encounters on the beach at Bembridge and over coffee in the early hours among the cabbies after the ball was over. I doubt whether all the proposals were entirely serious though some certainly were. Moreover she and her biographers all seem slightly unsure about whether it was forty-eight, forty-nine or fifty. It is difficult to see how one could offer objective proof on the matter.

'I think you ought to do my three big love affairs, don't you think so?' said Dame Barbara one afternoon on the sofa at Camfield Place. It wasn't entirely clear at the time whether these were pre-marital or post-marital. They certainly weren't marital and in the event they had about them the well-honed feel of good stories by a past-mistress of the romantic genre.

'The first', she said, 'was the Duke of Sutherland only he was already married. He was in love first of all with Lady Cynthia Curzon who was the most beautiful person. Then Duchess Millicent (the Duke's mother) told me herself that she said to him "You've got to marry, you've got to marry, you've got to have an heir", d'you see, because they were very short of heirs in Scotland. And so he said all right, but you choose because if I can't marry the woman I want I couldn't care. So she asked three girls to Dunrobin. And the first one was very, very good looking but she was a barren woman. And everyone has always said that Raine was his child but actually I never went to bed with him. You won't believe it but in those days one didn't.

'My mother made me swear I wouldn't have an affair with a married man. He used to come into my bedroom and lie on the bed and kiss me. I'd let him kiss me but I wouldn't let him get into bed with me. And therefore he loved me to the very end.' At the very end of the Duke's life they met at a luncheon party in London. The Duke's last wife turned to Barbara and said 'Of course, Raine is Geordie's daughter'.

'Well,' says Dame Barbara, 'I was so fed up with saying

"no, she isn't" that I didn't say anything. If I said "no" they wouldn't believe me. I was so fed up with the whole thing. But actually it wasn't at all because I never went to bed with him. But nobody believes that.'

So the Duke was evidently great love number one.

The second, she says now, was a man called Nigs. Incidentally, she adds in an aside, these beaux are all dead now so it doesn't matter what one says. Or to be more precise one can tell the truth and know that no one can get hurt. This is a compelling argument – perhaps the only one – for surviving one's nearest and dearest.

'I fell in love in the South of France,' she says, 'immediately after my divorce [1931] I think it was. I went to lunch with Maxine Elliott who had this wonderful place and she said I want you to play backgammon with Viscount, oh Viscount ... I can't spell his name, we shall have to look it up.' (We did. It was Rattendon.) 'And we fell in love like that' (she snapped her fingers). 'Really like that. But we were both doing time. *His* wife – now this is absolutely fascinating – was the daughter of Forbes Robertson, you know – and she ran off with his chauffeur and pilot, which was considered very down-market.'

It is interesting to see how this racy, matter-of-fact account of the romance compares with earlier versions. I had read about Nigs in Gwen Robyns but there was nothing in that account about Blossom Forbes-Robertson going off with the chauffeur. (Blossom incidentally only had one eye, a fact which Barbara ascribed to bizarre supernatural pre-natal influences. Her actress mother had spent seven months of her pregnancy playing the part of a one-eyed woman. So no wonder the wretched Blossom was born monocular!) She also told Gwen Robyns that she and Nigs had met in an earlier incarnation, though she didn't mention it to me. Horses for courses. I suspect she thought I'd sneer.

'Nigs and I were very much in love but we had to be frightfully careful. And then he said to me "I can't have any children".' While serving with the Bengal Lancers Nigs had contracted eczema. This was treated with radium and carried out in such a cavalier fashion that the man was rendered sterile and permanently unable to father children.

'He'd asked me to marry him the first night we were sort of . . . together. And I said "Oh". And, you know, time went by and we went and looked at houses, and I kept saying "do I want to be left with just one little girl" [Raine] – and I certainly didn't. So in the end I went away to Baden-Baden again and I wrote to him and everything and said that I thought the answer was "no". It had gone on for six months. And he then, in a "pet", said when I got back, "well I've found a girl who doesn't care and so I'm marrying her." Well it lasted six months. And to make the end of the story complete Somerset Maugham . . . on his wedding day he sent me an enormous bouquet of flowers and a letter. It was rather pathetic. On his wedding day. So it obviously wasn't going to be a success.

'I never saw him again until he was eighty-two and I was here. I said "come to lunch". And he'd married the sister of that woman. D'you remember . . . Erroll, the Happy Valley case in Kenya, I was all mixed up with them all . . . it's all in the film . . . anyhow, so I said "come to lunch" and she did. She was rather hostile until the boys gave her a lot to drink. He was just the same. I've always been in love with blue-eyed, fair-haired men who were rather stupid even though I've always written about dark-haired men with . . . well, never mind. When he was leaving he said "Barbara, I want to show you something in my car". So I went across to his car and he said, "There's the St Christopher you gave me."

'Darling, I couldn't remember I'd given it him. It was an awful end to the story. But that was a great romance really.'

The third great love, whom she says now she really ought perhaps to have married, was the son of Earl Beauchamp, Viscount Elmley. He had proposed to her when she was only eighteen or so and the match was much favoured by her mother Polly. The Beauchamps were Worcestershire county. There was money, a title, land, a grand house, everything poor Polly could have wished for her underprivileged daughter.

'I didn't really want to marry him,' Barbara recalled, recollecting the proposal from the safety of old age. 'He was awfully uncouth. He had a sort of thing . . . he used to shake occasionally when he was frightened. His father had been exiled by the King, if you remember, and he would attack the chauffeurs when one went to lunch. So you can't say it was very glamorous can you? Of course they did have the most wonderful house – Madresfield Court – and now, in Worcestershire, of course it's one of the best places in England with more value than anything else and a moat round it. I've written about it heaps of times. Anyway this went on and on and in the end I said "no" definitely.

'And we met at various times and when I kissed him it was horrible, and, you know, it just didn't work. And then he married a terribly nice woman and I used to go to lunch there and she used to say, "sit next to Elmley, he's always loved you more than anybody else." She used to say so, in front of people you know – it was pathetic. But, don't you see, you can't marry people, if you're me, unless you're really in love with them. That's the whole point and I think that should be made because' (the 'because' was given high emphasis) '. . . because so many people today say "oh, girls just marry anybody". And you must marry for love.

'They telephoned today,' she continued. 'They' was yet another of the newspapers who assail her daily for instant quotations on the subjects of the day. 'They' had wanted Dame Barbara's reaction to some new book on contemporary sexual mores. Dame Babara was predictably unamused.

I am not entirely clear about her attitudes to love and sex and I'm not entirely sure I find them altogether consistent. After all, she did not marry poor Nigs even though she loved him to death, but she had a relationship with Lord Elmsley even though she didn't fancy him at all and found his kisses 'horrible'.

The man from the newspaper had asked a 'silly question' that morning. He had asked her why she thought love important. She told him it was because love was holy. She had been doing some research for a new novel which involved finding out about Aphrodite, the Greek Goddess of love – or as she put it 'Venus before she was called Venus'.

'Girls', she explained, 'were dressed as nuns but they were actually prostitutes. They all had a service. And then the man had a service too and had to pray. Then they made love because it was real love. Don't you see. This was something real. Not this muck they have now. And, do you see, it's all ended in AIDS. I won't mention AIDS. I don't have anything to do with AIDS at all. I won't give money towards AIDS because I think the whole thing's disgusting. It only came on because of the queers as you know perfectly well.'

Now in all fairness this exposition took place after a heavy session dictating the new novel when the Dame was in her ninety-third year. Yet wherever I look in her writings and in her utterances over the years I find the same peculiarities and inconsistencies and downright muddle. Her attitudes are most certainly not, despite her background, those of the middle class Church of England. Mysticism and the Ancient Greeks play a far more prominent part in her beliefs than the Book of Common Prayer. Almost the only time she mentions the Bible is to refer to Genesis and the Garden of Eden. She seems more intrigued by Buddha and Yoga. She believes in reincarnation but not in the Christian sense. She thinks we come back in other forms – better or worse depending on the lives we have led this time round. But then friends and family also return to her in some sort of vision, some more than others.

She is a tremendous weaver of spells and talking in the 1990s on the sofa about these three old flames it was almost as if she was dicating one of her novels. It was difficult to be sure where fact and fantasy merged, how much was wish and how much fulfilment.

In telling me about these three great loves of her life she did not mention Alexander McCorquodale. This is not altogether surprising in view of what later happened, but I can't help wondering how much in love she was when Alexander, generally known as 'Sachie', proposed to her. She gives him no mention in *We Danced All Night* and in *The Isthmus Years*, her 'autobiographical study of the years between the two world wars', she says very succinctly: 'In the spring of 1927 I became engaged to be married to Alexander McCorquodale, whose father was chairman of the companies owning the largest printing group in England. It was the end of an era in my life.'

This is not the euphoric reaction to matrimony that one would expect from one of her own heroines. There is not much sign of ecstasy or even expectation. It sounds more like resignation.

Sachie, however, seems to have been in love with her. Gwen Robyns says that he was 'eminently eligible' which is true in the sense that he was single; that he was dark (though we know that real-life Barbara preferred blonds); that he was tall (well quite, in the wedding pictures he looks about the same height as his bride); and handsome (quite, I should have said – his hair looks a tad thin, his mouth ditto and his eyes are rather too close. His expression in the photographs that survive looks dour). He was also Scottish which Barbara has always found attractive but the McCorquodales were not titled. Indeed they were trade. Nothing wrong with printers but most of Barbara's smart friends married titles and the best Sachie could manage in this respect was an uncle called Lord Horne of Stirkoke who is always said to have 'commanded the First Army during the War'.

But the one factor which made Sachie McCorquodale a good catch for young Barbara was that he was indisputably rich. His father's company printed all the Government's postal orders and they had a grand house in Shropshire called Cound Hall.

Sachie was also a very fine game shot – nearly all Cartland heroines in fact and fiction are terrific with a twelve bore – a good salmon fisherman, also a plus; and was said to be experienced as far as women were concerned. Being good in bed is a prerequisite for both sorts of Cartland heroes (fact and fiction) but Barbara and Sachie did not of course sleep with each other before marriage. Had she done so, she admitted years later to Dr Anthony Clare 'In the Psychiatrist's Chair', she might have had second thoughts about Sachie. Her shrewd mother Polly was glad about the money though sad about the title. She wondered if he was 'worthy' of her and was afraid the McCorquodales might prove dull.

Never mind, Sachie promised Barbara a house in Mayfair and a Rolls Royce of her own. After almost a decade of penny-pinching and gold-digging she could become a society hostess in her own right. Perhaps she was not 'wildly' in love but she was sure it would all turn out for the best. 'I was quite determined', she told John Pearson in 1979, 'I would be a wonderful, wonderful wife.'

Chapter Five

She divorces. Four years later she
marries again.

T his Romance was short-lived.

More than sixty years after the event she still spoke bitterly about her divorce and particularly about the McCorquodales. They tried, in effect, to destroy her and they came close to doing so.

Her marriage was plainly a mistake. Alexander McCorquodale was not just the quiet, gentle, attractive man she loved and married, he was also a serious drunk. He spent long, solitary hours at his club before coming home and rather primly contenting himself with a half pint of pale ale. 'Hardly surprising,' she says, caustically, 'as he was sozzled after all the drink he'd had during the day.' Scarcely anyone realised that Sachie had a problem, not even his cousin and business associate, Hugh, who was one of his greatest friends. The two had been at school together and were good companions. Some people have suggested that drink had an adverse effect on Sachie's sexual performance.

One night at home in the house in Green Street, just off Park Lane, God came to the young Mrs McCorquodale, as he so often has in the course of her life, and told her that she should go down to Sachie's study where she would find something of interest.

She went downstairs and there in a drawer of his writing desk she found letters between her husband and a woman called Helene Curtis, wife of a Major Philip Pinckney Curtis. As the judge in the subsequent case was to remark, 'The letters seem to speak for themselves.' They contained all the usual sentiments you would expect of love letters with references to rapturous moments, lying in one another's arms and what the judge, with a definite suggestion of judicial distaste, referred to as 'matters of that kind'.

The most chilling passage of all, however, was a reference to her infant daughter, Raine, born in September 1929. The suggestion was that if both parties were careful and avoided any precipitate action they should both be able to retain custody of their children. Barbara's husband was plotting not only to set up with another woman but also, in effect, to abduct their daughter.

Barbara, outraged, took the letter to her in-laws but received scant sympathy.

Accordingly she sued Sachie for divorce, but to her amazement and distress Sachie did not do the decent thing and accept like a gentleman. Instead he filed a cross-petition of his own alleging that Barbara had been carrying on with Hugh.

The McCorquodales had money and they had clout. They were a powerful clan. However, Barbara, while fairly broke, nevertheless had a certain amount of clout of her own. She was already something of a celebrity – the *Evening Standard*, writing a description of the scarlet-and-gold, much-mirrored ostentation of the Mayfair house in 1931, remarked with prescience and a certain awe, 'She is an original in many ways.'

Her brother Ronald was a special help in this crisis. The

McCorquodales retained Norman Birkett KC, one of the great trial lawyers of the century. Ronald mentioned this to his friend, Sir Patrick Hastings KC, who had been attorney-general in the 1924 Labour government, and was one of the few barristers to rival Birkett. Hastings was outraged by the McCorquodales' behaviour, which he saw as typical of a rich, privileged aristocracy bludgeoning a poor, innocent, defence-less girl into distress and wretchedness. Hastings told Ronald that he would take on his sister's case for no fee.

With the involvement of these two KCs the case was bound to attract publicity. Divorce cases in those days were avidly reported and the best possible way of getting sex and scandal into supposedly respectable newspapers. This case lacked a good title – Barbara was no Duchess of Argyll – and there were no photographs or tape-recordings. But it had much else besides.

DIVORCE SUIT BY NOVELIST
HUSBAND'S CRUISE IN LINER
COUSIN CITED IN CROSS PETITION

Sachie conceded that he had indeed committed adultery with the major's wife aboard the SS *Homeric*. Dame Barbara says now that Sachie was always going on cruises aboard the *Homeric*, though not with her. McCorquodales did the printing for the White Star Line, which owned the *Homeric*, so he had a perfect excuse. Despite the *Homeric*, however, Sachie denied going to bed with Mrs Curtis either at Tyrcelyn, near Builth Wells, the home of her mother, Lady Windham, or at the Bongate Hotel in Appleby or the Three Arrows Hotel in Boroughbridge.

He also alleged that his wife had gone to bed with his cousin Hugh at a hotel in Loughborough when they were on their way to Derby where the three of them were to meet up and proceed to a joint holiday at Gleneagles. Hugh and

Barbara protested that there had been heavy fog that evening and they had been unable to continue. The following day they had gone on and the three of them went to Gleneagles where they enjoyed a happy holiday.

This was the only specific occasion, but almost more damaging were the revelations about the daily life in Culross Street. The *Daily Telegraph*, in a long, salacious but characteristically stuffy report, summarised the judge's view as being that 'the habits of the household were not, he supposed, the ordinary habits of a household as generally known'.

One rather supposes not. Hugh lived at the Bath Club but had his own latch-key. He was there at all hours of the day and night and would go to Barbara's bedroom where she would kiss him, call him darling and offer him cocktails. Her typically sprightly and all too plausible defence against this charge was that she offered all her friends cocktails in her bedroom. 'It was to be remembered', said the judge, Lord Merrivale, clearly impressed with this wronged wife, 'that Mrs McCorquodale was a literary woman with a high degree of mental capacity using her room as a study and a place in which to receive her guests.' Furthermore, 'Mrs McCorquodale said that she called most of her friends "darling" and kissed most of them, men and women.'

Lord Merrivale seems to have been much taken with Barbara and his summing up left little room for doubt as to whose side he was on. The McCorquodales produced the ex-butler Finney who said that one day he took tea in to his mistress only to find Mr Hugh 'sitting beside Mrs McCorquodale in a very familiar manner'. They also produced a former footman and 'a multitude of young women'. But neither the butler, nor the footman nor the young women were believed. Or if they were believed they were only believed to the extent that Hugh and Barbara were close friends and that Barbara's life-style was unorthodox. Even the admitted fact that Hugh had given her a diamond bracelet and a frock for Ascot seemed not to convince judge or jury that anything improper had taken place between the two of them.

'You have seen Mrs McCorquodale and you can judge whether she was the sort of woman who would throw herself into another man's arms in a profligate way,' said the judge.

The jury retired to think about this and needed only fifteen minutes for their deliberations. On returning they found that there had indeed been misconduct between Sachie and the Major's wife but that 'Mrs McCorquodale had not committed misconduct with Mr Hugh McCorquodale, her husband's cousin'.

Accordingly, Barbara got a decree nisi and costs. Just over four years later, quietly without fuss, she and Hugh were married. They enjoyed twenty-eight years of marriage during which time they were, in Dame Barbara's words, 'blissfully happy'. Second time round she had found the right cousin.

Chapter Six

Barbara is a mother. Raine is a celebrity.
Barbara writes thousands of words a day.
She is a pioneer glider and drives a racing
car. Her sons are born. She helps her brother
Ronald become an MP.

A divorced mother of one with no visible means of support was not an enviable person at the beginning of the Depression. The Mayfair mansion went and so did the Rolls Royce. In later life she never really spoke ill of Sachie, reserving her vitriol for his family. The divorce settlement left her with a mere five hundred pounds a year to live on. The meagreness of this offering she blamed on the meanness of the McCorquodales.

Little Raine seems to have been more of an encumbrance than an asset. She was 'tiresome' and 'delicate'. Her thymus gland was enlarged and would be a serious worry for the first four years of her life. Raine required a nanny, though part of the divorce settlement was that the horrible McCorquodales would pay for a nanny so that Barbara would be free to work and socialise. (Could this be the same Barbara who, in her nineties, campaigned so ardently for mothers to be paid a salary so that they could stay home where they belonged and look after their little ones?) Raine was not strong and suffered badly from eczema.

Raine's redeeming grace was that she could sometimes be a sort of fashion accessory. Even her birth was noted in the

Daily Sketch gossip column in a heavy-handed spoof of a race card with 'runners and weights'. Raine, at seven pounds ten ounces, came between Lady Alington's Mary and Lady Diana Cooper's Julius (now the writer John Julius Norwich). Mrs McCorquodale is, significantly, the only commoner among these society mums.

One observer noted later that the child had almost as many smart invitations on her dressing-table as her sociable mother. And the invitations *were* smart. In an article on 'Society Children', in 1933, *Vogue* suggested, archly, that 'her engagement diary must be almost as full as mother's'. One of Raine's first outings was a fancy dress party at Londonderry House to which she went, aged one, as a fairy.

A bubbly five year old came up to Nanny and said, 'Oh, what a lovely fat baby! What is her name?'

When Nanny said Raine the little girl remarked 'What a funny name'. A fair enough comment, if a little sharp. Characteristic, I should say, for the five year old was none other than Princess Elizabeth, now Queen Elizabeth II.

Baby Raine certainly seems to have moved in the very best circles right from the beginning. The unusual name, incidentally, is Gaelic in deference to the Scottish antecedents on both sides of the family. Barbara didn't think it funny at all. She chose it because she thought it romantic.

One got divorced. One's marriage failed. Yet the times, as the Dame of later life tried with such exasperation to explain, were so completely different. The end of a marriage was not the relatively commonplace affair it has become today. It was the end of the world. In her diary, the indomitable Polly wrote of her daughter's trouble, 'Bab's Case awful, two lives wrecked'. And in a sense her life did look wrecked. There was a stigma attached to divorce no matter how innocent one might be. It was not only the royal enclosure at Ascot that was barred to a divorced person, however innocent. People disapproved.

Life was particularly hard for the divorced but it was not easy for anyone much. People were suffering, even if some people's suffering was greater than others'. 'In 1932,' she wrote subsequently, 'times were bad for everybody and people were prepared to sell everything and anything. Commission was asked most unexpectedly even in an era when people had ceased to be surprised at any depths to which their friends and acquaintances would sink.'

Barbara's first novel, *Jigsaw*, had enjoyed something of a *succès de scandale*. However the astonishing fecundity with which we now associate her was still to come. In her first decade as a novelist she wrote less than one a year. There was no way in which she could maintain her standard of living by writing novels.

She was a prolific journalist, for the *Express*, for the *Observer*, for the *Tatler*, where she wrote a column called Panorama for three years in the mid-thirties under the name 'Miss Scott'. She also made a series of broadcasts from Savoy Hill on the subject of 'How to make the best of oneself'. They were supposed to be for 'the working woman'. Years later she actually met 'working women' and was ashamed of 'those bright, glib little talks'. She had been taken home in a Rolls after 'giving advice to women who were trying to feed and clothe a family on what it cost for two people at the Savoy'. These sudden flashes of self-awareness sometimes surprise but they do happen and they are endearing.

When times were most hard she says that she was writing as many as ten thousand words a day. It was this that paid the bills. Most of the essays in journalism, unlike the broadcasts of course, were anonymous. They tended to be society gossip and it was important to Barbara that no one should know that she was supplying the papers and magazines with inside information. And so, apart from Miss Scott, she was 'Miss Hamilton' under the Caviare column in the *Bystander* and 'Miss Tudor' in the *Daily Mail*. She was also for a while the social editress of the *National Graphic*. For a woman not obviously given to reticence she managed to keep her secret surprisingly well. Her employers were remarkably loyal. It is even alleged that the redoubtable Lady Astor was unable to persuade her son, Bill, to tell her whom he was paying to write the *Observer*'s social column. It seems impossible.

Just once, in 1933, she ventured out of the froth of society chit-chat. She described it with charming ingenuousness as having been 'what Fleet Street calls a "scoop"'. This was the story of 'The Prisoner in the Tower', Lieutenant Norman Baillie-Stewart. Baillie-Stewart was later court-martialled for selling British military secrets through a girlfriend called Marie-Louise. Barbara learned that Baillie-Stewart was incarcerated in the Tower of London through a well-connected friend. With the acumen of a true journalist she got on to J.B. Wilson, the news editor at the *Daily Express*, and the story was next morning's front-page lead. Even now, however, she will not reveal her source and although she was happy enough to take a fee of fifty pounds, her bye-line was not on the article. She preferred to remain an unknown tipster.

Nevertheless she was already displaying that famous flair for self-publicity when it suited her. Perhaps it is unfair to talk of publicity 'stunts' but there was a 'stuntish' quality to some of her escapades.

Take, for example, the business of the glider.

This was the day of Amy Johnson who flew to Australia solo in twenty days, a feat emulated by C.W.A. Scott in 1931. He did it in a mere nine. In Barbara's words, 'Flying was the main interest of the young and dashing', and instead of running down to the south of France for a weekend one 'hopped' across to Le Touquet in one's privately owned Puss Moth.

That summer of 1931 Barbara and a friend, the writer Ian Davison, 'became thrilled with the idea of towing a glider by aeroplane'. Their revolutionary idea was to tow a glider aloft behind a powered aeroplane. When they had attained enough height the glider would be released and would fly on to its destination. Barbara thought it might be feasible to have a whole train of towed gliders. Each one could be released wherever appropriate, rather like the old railway 'slip coaches'. Barbara and Ian Davison had two co-conspirators, Flying Officers Mole and Wanless.

To demonstrate the idea's feasibility the team decided to take a special glider up to ten thousand feet and then let it drift across the Channel to land at a French aerodrome. If it worked it would be a wonderfully cheap way of delivering airmail.

Shortly after the glider had been commissioned under what they thought were conditions of complete secrecy someone leaked the story to the *Daily Mail*. The *Mail* announced a one thousand pound prize for the first glider to fly both ways across the Channel.

Barbara was outraged, even more so when the manufacturer of her glider decided to go in for the competition himself. In her film treatment, 'I Follow My Secret Heart', she allows herself a splendidly vituperative little speech, saying, 'I think it is one of the most disgraceful things I have ever heard. It is extremely crooked of him considering I have already paid him five hundred pounds for the glider.'

In the end they abandoned the idea of the Channel and decided instead to take the first ever glider-towed mail from Manston airport to Reading. The glider, red and white, had the legend 'Barbara Cartland' emblazoned along the side. On 20 June Barbara and Flying Officer Wanless in the aeroplane towed Flying Officer Mole and the glider into the skies and launched him towards Reading.

All went well. The Mayor of Reading accepted the formal airmail letter; the Vice-President of the International Commission for the Study of Motorless Flight arrived from Heston with five planes and escorted the pioneers back to his airfield and the whole affair was a great success. That summer the 'Barbara Cartland' competed in several rallies, carried a passenger from London to Blackpool, convincingly out-racing the competing London to Blackpool railway express. Eventually she established a falling-flight record of four and three quarter miles before being blown over three times on landing. She was then consigned to the scrap-heap.

Shortly afterwards the Air Ministry banned aeroplane-towed gliders but the Germans persevered and during the war used them in the invasion of Crete. The Allies were slow to learn and didn't employ them until the Normandy landings. Even more belatedly, in 1984, this peculiar event was recognised when Barbara, aged eighty-three, went to Kennedy airport to receive the Bishop Wright Air Industry Award for her 'Contribution to Aviation'.

Interestingly enough, her professed reason for not competing in the *Daily Mail* challenge was that she was afraid 'the whole thing would be turned into a "stunt"'. As in other matters her attitudes are seldom consistent.

That same year, for instance, even though she disliked driving, she organised what she herself described as a 'news-stunt' at Brooklands. The idea was that a bevy of society beauties would drive supercharged MGs round the track 'ostensibly to show the public that women could drive as well as men – actually to publicise the cars'. In 1931 it was very difficult to find enough good-looking, well-bred girls who could drive supercharged MGs round Brooklands. But Barbara managed. She herself drove, partnered by Ted

(Lord) de Clifford 'who had married Mrs Meyrick's daughter'. Lady de Clifford, (Dorothy), 'partnered the winner, Princess George Imeretinsky, eldest daughter of Sir George Mullens, whose sister Mrs Barney was to be successfully acquitted of a murder charge in 1933 when defended by Sir Patrick Hastings'.

This is a statement of fact, but it is still 'essence of Barbara' and just another demonstration of the old adage about life being stranger than fiction. Even Cartland fiction would have a job to match this particular 'news-stunt', one of many of Dame Barbara's youth.

In truth she was ever a stuntswoman.

Her relative poverty in the years between her two marriages was tiresome because she had always enjoyed material comfort as well as attaching great inherited importance to keeping face and maintaining appearances. On the other hand she maintains, with characteristic gusto, that 'I've never lost a friend by being poor – I've gained them and only mislaid them when I got well off again'. She managed to have fun. She managed to have boyfriends including the Duke who got away.

In Angela Levin's book on Johnnie and Raine Spencer she quotes one 'member of the family' saying, cattily, 'Can you imagine Barbara turning down a title in the financial circumstances she was in?'

Well yes, actually. After all, neither of her marriages were to titled men even though they were both well-to-do. Inconsistent though she so often is, she was in many ways a genuinely incurable romantic and it seems improbable that she would have married a peer she didn't at least fancy.

In the event, as we have seen, she married Sachie's cousin Hugh, who had been cited by him in the divorce. The story is that Hugh had originally fallen in love with Barbara on her first wedding day but had been too much of a gentleman to say so, particularly as Sachie was not only his cousin but had been his best friend at school. Nevertheless that does not seem to have prevented him behaving in a fairly injudicious fashion during the early years of Barbara and Sachie's marriage while Sachie was away cruising on the *Homeric* with the Major's wife. All those kisses and cocktails in Barbara's bedroom may have been quite harmless but they were scarcely discreet.

Hugh was a war victim. Indeed after his death Barbara succeeded in avoiding any death duties on the grounds that he had died as the direct, if belated, result of enemy action. The wounds were sustained at Passchendaele where he won the Military Cross serving with the Cameron Highlanders. A sniper's bullet destroyed a lung and three ribs; he almost died there and then and was never in very good health although he lived on until 1963.

Dame Barbara says she 'adored' her husband Hugh but she doesn't speak a great deal about him at all. 'Like all McCorquodales,' she wrote, in *The Isthmus Years*, 'he was an expert fisherman and a first-class game shot.' (These two qualities were almost as important in a husband as being a Duke or even having money. They were absolute indicators that one had been properly brought up!)

Unlike practically every other event in her life, the second wedding was quiet to the point of anonymity. It took the form of a service at the Guildhall and a blessing in St Ethelburga the Virgin, Bishopsgate on 28 December 1936. Then they went off to honeymoon at the Carlton in Cannes – 'an ecstatically happy time'. One of the first people they bumped into was her old friend Wallis Simpson, by now, in Barbara's estimation, 'the most talked-about woman of the century'. She was also 'charming, unaffected and very gay'. It could never be said that, at least in adulthood, Barbara

Cartland has ever been anything other than exceedingly well connected. Privately, however, she is less flattering about Wallis whom she plainly considers rather 'fast'.

For years she had hankered for a son and this time her wish was granted with the utmost expedition. Ian arrived on 11 August the following year and was welcomed as 'the most exciting, wonderful thing that has happened to me' even though he was so beautifully like an angel that she was afraid he would die. Devoted though she was, her maternalism was not that much more in evidence than it had been with Raine. As Angela Levin observes, Ian was less than a year old when he was packed off to Granny while his father went fishing in Scotland and Barbara and her brother Ronald went to Switzerland together.

It is at least arguable that Ronald has been the single most significant person in Dame Barbara's entire life. She has said to me that Ronald and she had everything with the single exception of sex. She certainly seems to have preferred his company to that of everybody else in the world and throughout the thirties the two of them relied on each other to an exceptional degree.

They were close even before the divorce but the way in which Ronald came to his sister's aid, organised Sir Patrick Hastings for the defence, found her a place to live and generally provided solid moral support, could only serve to bind them even closer. However, it was his decision to stand for parliament which really cemented their relationship.

It happened on Tuesday 16 October 1933. After a day's work at Conservative Central Office he and Barbara met for a late tea and he told her that Major Beaumont-Thomas, the MP for the Birmingham constituency of King's Norton, was not going to stand again. It was the seat Ronald coveted most and Barbara immediately said he must put his name forward no matter what. She has always been inclined to impetuous if not quixotic gestures and still is, even in her nineties.

The trouble was that they were both as poor as each other and the election expenses would amount to almost a thousand pounds. He said she was mad; she said money didn't matter, their Faith would see them through. She has always been a great believer in the efficacy of Faith even though she sometimes seems unclear about precisely what it is.

They argued away for a couple of hours and eventually Ronald agreed to put his name forward despite the lack of funds. Next day Barbara found herself in a Scottish house party which included the MP Leo Amery, later famous for giving Neville Chamberlain his marching orders with the words, 'In the name of God, go!' Amery listened to Barbara's story and said, 'Never let money stand in the way of opportunity', a resonant aphorism though easier said than done.

Back in London Amery came to Barbara's house where he met Ronald and was sufficiently impressed to endorse his application to King's Norton.

By November, when Ronald and his mother – his mother! – went to meet the selection committee, he was already in poll position. Apart from Amery he also had the support of the First Lord of the Admiralty and the Chief Whip. The family associations, too, were crucial. There was a Cartland Road in the Constituency; his grandparents were interred in the vault of the parish church and there were a number of public buildings erected by his grandfather James. He may have been a Carthusian domiciled in London but he was also in a very real sense the local candidate. Despite the fact that the selection committee had already turned down twenty other candidates Ronald turned out to be a shoe-in.

The three of them, Ronald, Barbara and their mother, really were astonishingly close. 'I tell you *everything*,' wrote Ronald to his mother after the first selection meeting. Later when he was summoned to a second meeting he took his speech to Barbara who listened to it over and over again, coaching him in 'elocution and gestures'. All three went to the second meeting, dining beforehand at the Queen's Hotel with the Chairman of the Association, and Ronald then spoke, only once having to refer to his notes.

He was adopted unanimously. There followed one final formal hurdle. The three of them were staying at the Priory. After the meeting they stayed up talking about politics, life and the future until after 3 a.m.

Money was a problem but he put a bold face on it and his words to Polly carry echoes. Dame Barbara, who for various reasons is not quite as massively rich as some might think, talks in much the same way about money. 'The only pretence', he wrote, 'is if we pretend we are richer than we are. But there is no need to do that! All I say is do not let us *volunteer* the information as to quite how poor we are.' These are characteristically Cartland sentiments. In any case, he finished, they could always raise money by selling the house.

Barbara was passionate in her support of her brother and because he was passionate about his politics she shared that passion too. To this day she remains hugely political, lobbying everyone from John Major down incessantly and vociferously on a wide range of subjects mainly to do with women and the family. Her political enthusiasm derives largely, I think, from Ronald, though it has to be said that she has never quite shared his political acumen. A lifelong Conservative she has always seemed marginalised in later years, formidable but scarcely mainstream. Under different circumstances she might have been a remarkable Member of Parliament herself.

It is also worth remembering that though Barbara has been categorised as a 'snob' and though she has very definite ideas about whether or not people are 'common' and whether or not a man is a 'gentleman' she is no more consistent about this than anything else. And Ronald was positively hostile.

Soon after becoming the candidate he and Barbara went to Birmingham for a political dinner: 'The dinner was awful,' he wrote. 'Everyone terribly refined, all much too "upper class" to laugh or applaud. They were attentive and B. made a nice little speech but no one thanked us for coming and we were left to drift about talking to people who didn't want to talk to us.'

To get round the constituency Ronald decided he should have a motor car. This was something of a novelty in those days. Mother bought him as second-hand, bolt-upright Austin. Barbara paid for it to be painted white with a black hood. It was known throughout King's Norton as the 'Whisky Car' – Black and White Scotch being one of the more popular blends of the day.

Barbara was almost a constituency wife to him. She subsidised him; holidayed with him; and above all she buoyed him up with her unfailing optimism and gaiety. It was Barbara who hired a room above the Cheshire Cheese in Fleet Street so that the family could watch the Silver Jubilee procession. It was Barbara who put together a little book encapsulating their joint philosophy, though Ronald corrected and edited and even tried to rewrite large chunks, an exercise in which he was foiled by his sister. In Barbara's words it also 'put briefly the advice they gave to anyone who, questioning fundamental issues, felt depressed'.

Ronald, naturally less of an optimist than Barbara, called this section, 'Uplift – lesson one'.

A letter to his mother illustrates the sun and the moon

in their respective outlooks. It came shortly after the death in a motor-cycle accident of Lawrence of Arabia.

'I seem to have a great deal to do and little time to do it in. I feel depressed about the money side of it all too. B. optimistic – but alas I'm not. I feel sometimes like giving it all up and going into a monastery. Lawrence was right, of course, in eschewing the world.'

That same year Ronald and Barbara visited Berlin and Bavaria on holiday. They were appalled. 'You shall have my impressions later on,' he wrote home to Polly. 'They're much the same as B.'s – ugly women, masses of uniforms, crowds of fat, aggressive people.' It is somehow typical that Barbara's first impression should be the ugliness of the women. Nevertheless they were agreed also on three more significant conclusions – that the Germans hated the English, that they would annex Austria and 'ultimately, and sooner than anyone expected, they would fight Great Britain'.

From this moment on Ronald, supported by Barbara, became one of the most outspoken political opponents of appeasement. He also maintained a simple philosophy which is very much Barbara's too and which was articulated in a curious almost Messianic election meeting with his Socialist opponent, G.R. Mitchison, husband of the writer Naomi.

'In this uncertain, dangerous, difficult world I am certain of only two things; my faith in God and my faith in the English people. There is an instinct in us – our greatest heritage – for what is right and for what is noble. In times of trouble, and in times of happiness, it has never failed us. We have so much to be thankful for, so much to do. God grant that you and I – and England – will never fail.'

This is positively Churchillian stuff. But given the extraordinary sibling relationship between Ronald and Barbara I wonder how much of her is in it too. And also how much of the sentiment and the style was born all those years before when Barbara sat at the feet of Beaverbrook, Churchill and F.E. Smith.

As the election neared Barbara and her mother seem to have devoted practically all their energies and resources to supporting Ronald's candidature.

Barbara, who had had a successful year of journalism, paid Ronald's deposit of a hundred and fifty pounds and guaranteed him an overdraft of three hundred pounds. No mean feat in those days. On 4 November when the campaign began in earnest Ronald moved into the Priory with his great-aunt, Annie, but as she had suffered a stroke and the house was full of nurses Polly and Barbara moved into a small local hotel.

It was they who became pre-eminent in Ronald's campaign. Mitchison was supported by the Labour Party's big guns such as George Lansbury and Stafford Cripps. Ronald was anxious to secure the Liberal vote since the local Liberal patrons – the well-disposed Cadbury family – had agreed not to run a candidate against him. Besides, he argued that Birmingham was not Conservative but rather Unionist country. Most people were too radical to warm to Conservative speakers from the south and the shires.

Therefore Ronald decided that he would not attempt to counter men like Lansbury and Cripps with politicians who punched a similar weight. Instead he turned to Polly and Barbara. Polly and Barbara canvassed all day. At night they would precede Ronald on to the platform, open the meeting, warm up the audience, and then rush on to the next venue as soon as Ronald got up to speak.

It sounds like a wonderfully fresh and inventive campaign. Ronald never descended to personalities, he was always courteous, but he knew his stuff. HECKLERS SILENCED IN THREE MINUTES ran one *Birmingham Evening Dispatch* headline. Even Labour supporters praised his fairness and candour. On one occasion a Scottish heckler complained that ten minutes' question time was far too short when the candidate was seeking a job for the whole of the next five years. Ronald immediately offered the man a lift in the 'Whisky Car' so that he could continue his questions at the next meeting.

The offer was accepted.

It rained on polling day. Labour were sure of success. Ronald, Polly and Barbara reached the Town Hall at midnight to find their opponent already there with Naomi, hatless and wearing high Russian boots.

At ten to one the result was declared. It was a famous victory for the Cartland family. Ronald had a majority of 5,875 votes.

Chapter Seven

Barbara throws herself behind her brother's political struggles. He is one of Mr Churchill's young men. There is a second World War. Two more family tragedies occur.

Portrait of Barbara in 1930.

*Barbara has always
enjoyed dressing up.
She has also had
a lifelong romance
with the camera.*

Barbara weds

. . . and divorces.

At the christening of her son Ian, in 1937.

Barbara with her children, Ian, Glen and Raine, in 1944.

At the christening of Raine's daughter Charlotte, in 1963.

With Raine and her third husband, Jean-François.

*Barbara and books:
her own armful,
and, in war,
books for the boys.*

Barbara, the writer at her desk at home.

D ame Barbara has always
been a complex and contrary creature. There are moments
when she seems to be fighting a female cause with such vigour
that she might pass for a feminist or at least a suffragette, but
other occasions when she appears to detest other women with
a shrill contempt from which the most misogynist male would
flinch; times when she displays a steely determination which
could only be – in her book(s) – masculine yet others when
she comes across, or seeks to, as a pink confection no more
substantial than candy floss.

Her association with Ronald and with his political career
seems to me to demonstrate her at her most sincere and most
impressive. There have been other successes, even triumphs,
some of them political, but there has never been a period in
her life when she has seemed quite so self-effacing, dedicated
and professional. Her belief in Ronald and what he stood for
appears total and she worked for him and for it quite selflessly.

From the first he was a fully paid-up member of the
awkward squad. Speaking, for instance, about what was
known in Birmingham as 'The Chamberlain tradition', he
remarked caustically, 'I wonder how many of those who so

glibly use those words, who are so pleased to reap the benefits that result from that tradition, understand what it means or do anything to keep it alive in the changed circumstances of the times. I am appalled by the lack of volunteers in the city for social and public service; I am dismayed by the seclusion from public services of those who are most fortunately situated.'

One may not always agree with what Dame Barbara has said or done in later life, whether through the St John's Ambulance Brigade or on behalf of the gypsies or young mothers or health foods and honey, but there is no disputing her dedication, no way in which you could accuse her of joining in 'the seclusion from public services of those who are most fortunately situated'. When the Labour Party complained because he was asked to open a fête to which they were not even invited he protested that, 'I regard myself as representative of every person in King's Norton, quite irrespective of their politics.'

His sister has remained a Conservative throughout her life but her Conservatism was as unorthodox as her Christianity and it has never been sectarian or exclusive. She always treated people the same, 'irrespective of their politics'.

During Ronald's years in the House of Commons he and Barbara continued to meet almost daily and they telephoned each other every single day on the dot of twenty minutes past nine. Throughout his parliamentary career he would discuss his every major speech with Barbara and draft it according to her comments. Then when he had completed a draft he would invariably read it through to their mother.

Like the Prince of Wales he visited South Wales and like the Prince he was infinitely depressed by what he found. One night he stayed at a settlement in the valleys and spent some time talking to the unemployed, most of them from the mines. Barbara asked if he thought he had done any good.

'Only', he said, 'in the fact that I showed them a Tory MP could be human. They had never seen one before and they expected a stout, pompous old gentleman with a heavy gold watch chain.' At twenty-nine he was far from that. He attached as much importance to a stylish appearance as his sister but his was not that sort of style.

The two remained virtually inseparable even after Barbara's second marriage. Hugh – brave, solid, shooting-and-fishing Hugh – suited Barbara well but Hugh did not scintillate the way Ronald did. She would rather spend time with Ronald than anyone.

In 1936, the year she married Hugh, she and Ronald holidayed together in Brittany. She liked to sleep a lot on holiday and one night was woken by chatter beneath her window. Opening it with a flourish she called out, 'unabashed by a Brighton accent': *'Silence! Silence! C'est après midi.'*

'It was a long time before Ronald allowed me to live that down.'

Ronald wrote regularly, as always, to their mother: 'We live in our bathing dresses except for meals when in true British style we appear *decently* clad – I in linen trousers and shirt, B. in a variety which puts the French to shame.'

And again, 'Every day B.'s and my voracious reading continues – a book a day being our average. Absurd? I agree, but we do enjoy it, and our taste varies from high spirituality to low sensuality.'

They sound impossibly close. The next letter home read in part, 'We adore your letters and there is great rivalry as to whom you write. I think B. and I are now all square. Last holidays B. complained bitterly you wrote to me more often than you wrote to her. What it is to have such devoted children that they even fight amongst themselves and with you for your epistles.'

Before her marriage to Hugh Ronald wrote to Barbara:

Darling,

I must send you this morning all my love and thoughts and
good wishes for the future. You know what you have meant to
me these last five years – much more than I can ever hope to
tell you – support, inspiration, courage, faith and love – I've
sought them from you often, never in vain. Now, after today,
it can't be quite the same – our relationship. But I'm not
unhappy about it. I'm glad. Because I know you are doing the
right thing, the wise thing, and the thing that is going to make
you happier and even more lovable to all of us in the future.

He went on to say nice things about Hugh, then added,
'Don't ever lose the memory of these last few years; the
struggles as well as the victories – and don't forget darling,
all the happy hours we've spent together. I don't think they're
finished.'

Indeed they were not. Almost immediately Hugh was
pottering off to Scotland for a spot of fishing on his own
while Barbara and Ronald went to the Continent much as
before. Even before that, when Barbara was pregnant with
Ian, Ronald spent two weeks with her in a rented house on
the Sussex coast while Hugh was in Scotland. The stay was
nearly a disaster for Ronald, much addicted to 'cheap' meals,
had bought a ham sandwich at the station buffet and arrived
almost crippled with food poisoning.

Barbara also continued to be a staunch political ally,
still, as always, helping out in every way, not least by
networking with him as they had always done together. All
their lives they made a habit of introducing each other to
friends who, like Sir Patrick Hastings or Leo Amery, were
to be instrumental in great sea-changes in their lives. One
year for instance Ronald wrote to his great-aunt Mary:
'My Youth Demonstration goes very well. I've raised fifty
pounds from our list of friends you and I drew up, and

Barbara's friend, Lady Waddilove, gave me five hundred pounds.'

Somehow Barbara always seems to have known a Lady Waddilove good for a few hundred pounds for her week's good cause.

In the summer of 1938 they were on holiday together without Hugh and without Barbara's children who were with Granny at Pevensey Bay. 'A rough crossing. B. felt ill,' wrote Ronald to 'Dear Darling' Polly. Then, 'We knew the hotel was "not us" – single rooms, no creature comforts. B. made up her mind at once. We went after breakfast.' In the next letter, 'an immense walk . . . it's a three-and-a-half-hours' walk and we did it in two and a half, B. protesting – and I'm not surprised. . . . I said we read. B. has just informed me she has read twenty-one books since she has been here. I have devoured ten. So you see our lives are not idle. The difference in the above figures is chiefly due to our difference in taste.'

Back in England Parliament was recalled to deal with the crisis in Czechoslovakia. When Chamberlain announced he was going to Munich to see Hitler, 'Ronald', in Barbara's words, 'was calm, silent and aloof in the midst of what was to him undignified emotionalism.' To Barbara he remarked, 'Do you think the Prime Minister is praying as he goes? No man needs more help from God.' When the Prime Minister returned with his piece of paper Ronald said, 'I rose very slowly to my feet. I did not cheer.' Noël Coward, a friend of both Barbara and Ronald, remarked to him, 'Neville Chamberlain has just discovered what every chorus boy discovers his first year on stage – the heady quality of applause.'

Ronald's opposition was not always popular. At lunch one day Barbara was shocked when one of her fellow guests said to her, 'Those traitors – Winston Churchill, your brother, and his like – should be shot.'

As a leading member of the small rebel group within

the Conservative Party, as well as an assiduous constituency MP and a tireless campaigner on behalf of the unemployed and disadvantaged, Ronald had an ever increasing work-load. At the beginning of 1939 Barbara persuaded him to move from his two small rooms in Petty France into a larger flat in the same building. Once more Barbara would pay the rent for, despite an increase in parliamentary salaries and a burgeoning income from his broadcasts and written articles, he was far from rich. Unfortunately his immaculate appearance led people to assume that he was and this sometimes got him into trouble. When he failed to make a substantial contribution to one of the Birmingham newspapers' Christmas Tree fund the editor took umbrage. But the fact was that Ronald could not afford it. To a certain extent the same problem has dogged Barbara. Because she values style and panache she sometimes looks richer than she really is. This does not always make her popular.

Ronald, in 1939, was still a young man and widely tipped as a future Prime Minister. Nevertheless his outspoken opinions, his regular defiance of the party whips, and his aggressive style made him enemies, particularly among older politicians within the House and in the constituency.

To Barbara he complained, 'They say I'm making mistakes – if I can't make mistakes at thirty-two when can I make them? And remember, when I am forty-five, the average age to start a political career, most of those in power will be dead or gone.'

In the end, of course, he and his colleagues, most prominent among them being Churchill, Eden, Macmillan and Leo Amery, were proved all too right. Any attack on appeasement was seen as an attack on the Conservative party, the Government and the Prime Minister himself. Ronald hated the way in which Chamberlain seemed to personalise everything and he also hated what he regarded as the 'pre-1914' way in which

Chamberlain – unlike the Cartlands' friend and hero Stanley Baldwin – jeered and sneered at the Labour party.

'It's unfair and it's undignified,' he complained to Barbara. 'To begin with the Socialists are a very small body. Neville can afford to be generous. Secondly, such behaviour is not becoming in a Prime Minister. The latter's job is to be the Father of the House – to be in a position, should the need arise, to call for unity and to get it. Neville is continually rubbing salt in the wound, he infuriates the Opposition – they would never follow him – he would never have their support even if the Germans were landing in Dover!'

His dislike of Chamberlain's policies, which teetered on the brink of personal antipathy and even contempt, was made worse by the fact that Chamberlain's was the next-door constituency to Ronald's and the Chamberlains were the city's most famous political family. Ronald's attitude was not calculated to win friends either within the party hierarchy or his own association.

Later, the journalist Beverley Baxter wrote to Barbara, 'I was in his constituency the other day. As you know, his outbreak against Chamberlain caused them great distress and, in fact Ronnie was in high disfavour. Now, however, since he has been proved right and since his actions in the war have been so brave, he has become a man with a halo.'

Ronald finally went over the top politically on the night of 2 August 1939. The Prime Minister was moving the adjournment of the House until 3 October. The Churchill faction argued that this was wholly irresponsible. The position vis-à-vis Hitler was far too dangerous.

A little later, after all-night manoeuvres with his Army unit, an artillery battery of the Worcester Yeomanry, he motored down to Caister-on-Sea where Barbara had taken a house for the summer. There he told her what had happened. Chamberlain and his supporters had made 'jeering, pettifogging party speeches'.

Depressed, Ronald and his friends made their way from the Chamber to be joined shortly by Churchill himself.

'Well,' Ronald said to him, 'we can do no more.'

'Do no more, my boy?' said Churchill. 'This is the time to fight – to speak – to attack.'

'I went back into the Chamber', Ronald told his sister, 'and when Geoffrey Mander sat down I was called – I regret nothing – I would say it again – I stand by everything I said. And when war comes – and come it will – the Prime Minister will be unable to unite the House, they will never follow him. And without a united Parliament you cannot have a united Nation.'

It was a blistering attack.

More than fifty years afterwards his old friend, Bill Deedes, could quote the most memorable phrase verbatim and straight off: 'We are in a situation that within a month we may be going to fight and we may be going to die.'

At this point an Hon. Member said, presumably derisively, 'Oh!' whereupon Ronald rounded on him and said with passion, 'It is all very well for the Hon. Gentleman to say "Oh". There are thousands of young men at the moment in training in camps, and giving up their holiday, and the least that we can do here, if we are not going to meet together from time to time and keep Parliament in session, is to show that we have immense faith in this democratic institution.'

He went on to add, 'I frankly say that I despair when I listen to speeches like that to which I have listened this afternoon.'

The result was predictable. He was applauded for his 'earnest, deeply felt speech' by Willie Gallacher, the Glaswegian communist MP. Then his Conservative neighbour, Sir Patrick

Hannon, said 'as I was partly responsible for getting him [Ronald] in his present seat I am bound to apologise to you, Mr Deputy Speaker, and to the House for the poisonous quality of the speech he delivered this afternoon.'

Uproar. Sir Patrick Hannon was repeatedly interrupted by MPs including Sir Richard Acland, Michael Foot and Brendan Bracken. But Ronald had said what he said and he had meant every word. Moreover he had said it at full throttle. When he did that the impact was often greater than he had intended.

Later, when people said to Barbara 'I was there, it was not what he said but the way he said it', she knew exactly what had happened.

'It was the old story of the "loudspeaker" being turned on too loud. This time the Members of Parliament had been "blasted out of their seats".'

The final act is all too predictable. Barbara was pregnant with her second son, Glen, and living by the sea. Ronald spent a euphoric few days lying on the sands reading a new book by the military historian, Basil Liddell-Hart, visiting Ely and Norwich cathedrals and playing with the children.

Then came a quite agreeable period of phoney war, home leaves, letters from France.

Finally Dunkirk, 1940.

A brother officer eventually wrote to say what happened:

All our guns were out of action and word had been given to make for the coast. On 30 May at about 8.30 a.m. we were about twenty miles from Cassel making our way about two miles east of Watou along a ditch bordering a lane, but we were not moving very fast as mist was rising and the country was getting open.

Ronald called me forward. While with him we saw German tanks going into action against other troops half a mile ahead. We decided to conceal ourselves, but later three tanks converged on us and we had to get up. As

Ronald rose he was hit in the head by a bullet and killed instantly.

Not far away their younger brother Tony was also killed. He was never as close and had spent much of his young adult life soldiering in Egypt. The blood ties were there but he was not a surrogate twin in the way that Ronald had been. He was surrounded and outnumbered, given the chance to surrender, refused, was wounded and finally killed by a shot from an automatic rifle. His last words were, 'I will surrender only unto God.'

'What a waste it all is,' Ronald wrote in his last farewell letter to Barbara, 'but after months of desolation we shall gain or retain what you and I have always understood the meaning of – freedom.'

More than fifty years later Ronald still came to his sister in her dreams or, she says, in visions. In 1993 she saw him as clearly as she saw me in the drawing-room at Camfield Place. Only later did she realise it was the anniversary of his death.

To lose two brothers and a father in the two world wars is grim but not, I suppose, unique.

To lose Ronald was a truly searing tragedy, a hole in her heart for ever.

Chapter Eight

*Barbara takes the children to Canada to escape
the war. Feeling remorseful she returns. She
becomes a Welfare Officer. She provides white
wedding dresses for our girls. She writes a
marching song for the St John's Ambulance
Brigade. At the end of the war she is not
even rewarded with 'a measly MBE'.*

Barbara Cartland has seldom been one to hide her light under a bushel and in her view she had a good war. Such a good war indeed that she afterwards exclaimed that 'When the War ended I ought to have been made a Dame, but actually there was only one measly MBE – for which I was the runner-up – given for the whole of the Honorary Welfare Officers to the Services'.

She had to wait the best part of half a century until she was almost ninety before she was finally made a Dame but she got there in the end, almost as much by sheer bloody-minded stamina as anything else.

In the years immediately before the outbreak of war, years she designated *The Isthmus Years* she was, as I've described, closely, indeed passionately, involved with her brother and his politics. However, she had married again, she had the two boy children she craved, she was a prolific if largely anonymous society gossip columnist and she continued to write books. These were more various in content and style than today although there were many fewer of them. Her seventeenth novel was finished shortly before the birth of Ian in 1937 – fourteen years after the first. This is prolific by conventional standards but not by those of the latter-day Dame.

Her life-style was affluent, or as she puts it 'comfortably-off'. Hugh was not as rich as cousin Sachie but he was a man of substance. Besides, after the trauma of the divorce she had resolved never to be completely dependent on anyone again. Hence the copious scribblings in the press. Also an open letter to poor Raine, then aged twelve, in which she admonished her, 'You are learning that money is unimportant and only brings happiness when you give it away . . . nearly every rich person I know is desperately unhappy; their money chains, encompasses, and often embitters them.'

Nevertheless there was a town house in St James's Square, later leased to General Eisenhower for the duration, and subsequently sold to Sir Bernard and Lady Docker, King and Queen of the post-war gossip columns. Lady Docker hid her jewels in the cistern of the loo, boasted of the fact and, naturally, had them stolen by newspaper-reading villains. This caused Barbara to remark reprovingly that if one was sensible one kept one's most valuable possessions in the bank.

Shortly after their marriage in 1936, Hugh and Barbara had bought a four-hundred-year-old thatched cottage at Great Barford in Bedfordshire. In the thirties it was a week-end retreat where they uncovered old beams, watched flowers grow on the banks of the Ouse and had passed what sound like gentle, idyllic hours. 'Happiness', she wrote, at her most lyrical, 'has no history and there is little to say of the hours we spent there, not dreaming it was later to be the only roof over our heads during the long, dreary years of war.'

As it happened the original idea was that Barbara and the three children should spend the 'dreary' war years well away from the action in Canada. After the fall of France Barbara had a call from Irene Dunn, wife of her old friend the Canadian millionaire, Sir James. She had a spare cabin aboard the liner which was to take her home and if Barbara could let her know by the following morning . . .

There followed a night of anguished deliberation, staring down at sleeping babies in cots, contemplating the Prime Minister's insistence that Britain was to be turned into an armed fortress, all women and children evacuated, forcibly if need be.

Then, finally, 'I looked across the room at my husband. I saw in his face the answer to the question we were asking ourselves. He needed no words to augment the pain in his eyes.'

So Barbara rang Irene Dunn, said yes please, went to the Passport Office, paid the bills, made sure the dog was going to be looked after, said goodbye to family (not many left alas), and friends (not as many of those as she'd thought), and after much bureaucracy and confusion, boarded the *Duchess of Atholl* in Liverpool.

'Nanny', however, 'was wonderful.' Dame Barbara has always been gracious and thankful to her nannies. And she has been singularly gracious to this particular nanny for her part in the great Canadian adventure. Had it not been for such nannies she would have had to spend much more time looking after her children and had less time for her professional life. This is perhaps worth remembering when she delivers one of her diatribes about the perils of the working mother. Despite what she wants for other women Barbara's place has never been altogether in the home, although in fairness she has always worked from home.

The passenger list on the *Duchess of Atholl* sounds inevitably Mayfair, and included Syrie Maugham and Tilly Losch, then the Countess of Carnarvon, among others who would have done credit to any of Barbara's social diaries.

However, despite being pampered on arrival in Montreal

by the fabulously rich, and generous Jimmy Dunn, Barbara was unutterably miserable. Both Ronald and Tony had been posted as 'missing' just as her father had been in the First World War. Her sense of loss was made almost worse by the uncertainty. She pined for her mother. She pined for England. . . . She felt 'an unreasoning blind despair, I felt trapped and desperate, helpless and utterly despondent'. Yet Ronald had always loathed people who 'made scenes in public and showed emotion before strangers' so she felt she simply must keep her upper lip stiff as he would have expected.

But she wanted to go home.

Before long this homesickness was compounded by a sense of guilt. So many ships were being sunk in the Atlantic that, by the end of July, it was obvious that the plans for a mass sea-evacuation of Britain were impractical. Then a ship, the *City of Benares*, was sunk with the loss of many lives, including children's. A mere seven thousand children, nearly all of them from well-to-do and privileged families, had been evacuated to Canada, Australia and South Africa when all plans for such evacuation were halted. Barbara thought of what her old acquaintance Winston Churchill had said about this being Britain's 'finest hour' and she decided that if indeed this was her country's finest hour then she was going to be part of it. Likewise her children. If poor people's children could put up with bombing then so could hers.

Having decided that it had been a mistake to come to Canada she responded with characteristic impetuosity. She cabled Hugh. She wrote to Hugh. He was to get Jim Thomas, the MP for Hereford, to intercede with Anthony Eden; he was to see Vincent Massey, the Canadian Minister in London; he was to see Sir Thomas Inskip, Secretary of State for the Dominions; he was to see her old friend and Ronald's mentor, Leo Amery, now Secretary of State for India; he was to see the heads of every shipping line.

If all this failed he was to see Churchill himself and convey the simple message that Barbara had made a mistake and she and the children wanted to come home immediately. 'I was furious with myself for coming away,' she said later, 'mainly because I was ashamed.'

It took time to get the necessary permissions to return. Finally, however, she got to see J.W. McConnell, President of the Montreal Star group of papers and McConnell interceded directly with the Canadian Under-Secretary of State for External Affairs. Despite the fact that the Canadian government had passed a law forbidding any of their ships from carrying women and children an exception was made for Barbara, presumably on the not unreasonable grounds that she was not a woman in the accepted sense. Also that, despite undertaking some highly successful lecture tours explaining the plight of Britain to Canadian audiences, she was managing to make a considerable nuisance of herself.

So in a blizzard in mid-November, she, the children and Nanny, were on board the *Duchess of Richmond*, a sister ship to the *Duchess of Atholl* in which they had arrived just a few months before. They had no idea of where they were to dock and were not allowed to send details of their ship for fear of any such message being intercepted by the enemy. Barbara's code was taken, appropriately, from *Debrett*. She wired her husband, 'Look at the Gordon-Lennox family tree', presuming (optimistically I would have thought) that no one in German codes and ciphers would be aware that the family name of the Duke and Duchess of Richmond was Gordon-Lennox. It was a message worthy of one of her novels.

They had no escort, guns which could only fire sideways and were useless fore-and-aft. Raine kept leaving her lifebelt in her cabin. Somehow Barbara managed not to be seasick though whether through fear or copious whisky-sours no one was sure. Diana Duff-Cooper always told her fear was the best anti-seasick pill. Barbara, however, thought it was the whisky-sours (equal parts rye whisky, lemon juice and white of egg) – 'the infallible nursery remedy for sickness'.

They docked at Liverpool a week later and Hugh was on the quayside.

Barbara's first words to him were, 'Can you get an ambulance, darling?' Ian had not slept all night and was breathing oddly. He had pneumonia.

The ambulance arrived, Ian recovered, Barbara passed through customs, declaring a dozen pairs of silk stockings and prepared to play her part in Britain's finest hour.

It was a curious part.

Luckily their tenants in Bedfordshire 'behaved extremely well' and moved out of the house within three days of Barbara's return. 'Extremely well' sounds like an understatement.

Almost as soon as they moved back into the cottage she succumbed to what she thought was cancer but which turned out to be a more or less benign abscess, though the operation to remove it caused excruciating pain and consequent bad language which shocked the surgeon. A longish convalescence ensued during which she began a novel, her twenty-second. She had had two published during the war, one of which, *The Black Panther*, embodied the idea of reincarnation, a notion which preoccupied her for the rest of her life. Indeed the one recurring question, to which she always seemed to expect an intelligent answer as one sat agog on the sofa at Camfield Place, was to do with how long it took someone to achieve reincarnation and what age one was when one returned. I think she thought that the older you were in your first life, the longer it took you to reach the second, but I'm afraid I always found the question totally perplexing and either gave unsatisfactory answers or, more usually, none at all.

As soon as she had recovered she asked the County Organiser of the Women's Voluntary Services, the Hon. Pearl Lawson Johnston, what war work she could do. The Hon. Pearl said she could take on the distribution of books in Bedfordshire.

For several months, Barbara, chauffeured by a Mrs Logsden, head of the WVS in Great Barford, drove chaotically about a Bedfordshire from which all signposts had been removed in order to frustrate German invaders and attempted to distribute people's cast-off books and magazines to squaddies in new and unmarked searchlight units, camps and aerodromes.

The WVS were competing for these books with the Merchant Navy and the Salvage. She obviously found the work frustrating.

'Could the Victorians really have written so many dull, stodgy novels?' she asked. 'What was the use of a guidebook to Germany at this particular moment, or of an empty and very damaged stamp album. Tracts arrived by the dozen, and heavily bound volumes of sermons must have been cleared from hundreds of shelves.'

Nevertheless the troops seemed pathetically grateful for this dubious reading matter. The only complaint she could recall was from a superior young sergeant who was sarcastic at finding among his gift volumes a copy of *Eric or Little by Little*.

Of all the books she received only about ten per cent, she thought, were worth reading. The most shining exception was a consignment of travelling libraries from the Pilgrims' Trust in America. These were a joy to distribute but unfortunately she found that 'people are, as a whole, fundamentally dishonest about books and umbrellas'.

Books went missing by the shelf-load.

From being, in effect, librarian to the services in Bedfordshire it was an easy and obvious step to becoming a Welfare Officer. These were volunteers under the command of a senior officer – in her case a Colonel Waley-Cohen – who were supposed to deal with 'everything which affected the individual serving man and woman personally, from a divorce to a draughtsboard'. From the autumn of 1941 onwards these Welfare Officers could accept honorary commissions and in December that year Barbara was gazetted an Honorary Junior Commander with the ATS. She was the only female Welfare Officer in the county and it is no surprise that her uniform was not common-or-garden Army issue but was tailor made by Worth. To her, it made perfect sense. After all Worth had her measurements and they gave her a special price.

One or two of her colleagues with chips on their shoulders were given to making disparaging remarks about this assumed affectation. One even said, 'I hear, McCorquodale, that you call all the Generals darling.'

To which she replied tartly, 'Only the men.'

As an Honorary unpaid officer Barbara was able to operate outside the rules of the hierarchy, though I think it is safe to say that she would not have been tied down by the rules under any circumstances anyway. She therefore felt that if some middle-ranking bureaucrat at the War Office did something silly she was perfectly entitled to go over his head to whoever she liked. For example, there was the case of a woman in the ATS who was married to an overworked and understaffed local farmer.

Barbara felt she should be released on compassionate grounds and was so outraged when the War office refused this on three separate occasions that she wrote personally to Lord Croft at the War Office, to R.S. Hudson the Minister for Agriculture and to Malcolm MacDonald the Under-Secretary at the Ministry of Labour. All wrote back polite but anodyne letters which appeared to pass the buck, but eventually the War Office retried the case and the woman was released. Barbara thought, candidly, that they got bored with her insistence. It was easier to acquiesce.

After a while Waley-Cohen asked her to take on the welfare of all the RAF in the county and she really came into her own. She could enjoy doing two of the things that she had learned to enjoy with Ronald – helping the under-privileged and tweaking the nose of authority. So when she discovered that three hundred newly arrived WAAFs had a recreation room with only three deck-chairs to sit in, she was in her element.

But her greatest triumphs were camiknickers and white wedding dresses.

'How I loved the RAF,' she said. 'They were so nice, intelligent, flexible-minded and ready to experiment.'

Appreciative as well.

After the war she encountered a senior officer who had served at RAF Cardington, formerly home of the great airships which came to an end with the crash of the ill-fated R101 – the vast hangers were still there in the 1990s.

'I well remember the difference you made to morale on the station just by providing the right sort of underwear which made our girls feel good,' he said. 'Or is that the wrong word?'

It was one of her first victories over the dreaded 'Authority'. Wartime rationing decreed that women in the Services should only have twelve or fourteen coupons with which they were supposed to buy handkerchiefs. One, or rather Barbara, could hardly imagine anything more ludicrous. The restriction was obviously thought up by a man (men are not *always* wonderful!) and agreed to by one of the 'Controllers', a title she hated and whom she described as 'de-sexed' and 'strident'.

Barbara, being Barbara, understood the importance of 'all the ravishing things which make a woman feel seductively feminine when it is next to her skin'. With the aid of a sympathetic Wing Commander she found a loophole in the regulations regarding Handicraft. Provided the purchase could be shown to be for 'recreational purposes' women could, she discovered, buy as much rayon, georgette, crêpe de Chine or other exotic material they could lay their hands on.

By the end of the war Barbara had personally bought almost ten thousand pounds' worth of materials and sold them by the yard to WAAFs all over Bedfordshire. 'All of them sported the most glamorous camiknickers under their uniforms.'

Glamorous camiknickers led to sex which led to marriage. That at least was the Cartland theory.

However, the white wedding dress was unquestionably an issue of the day and Barbara had considerable sympathy with those young ATSs compelled to get married in hideous khaki, particularly when she thought of the brides in white of her youth – such romantic figures as Margaret Wigham, Mary Malcolm, Lady Pamela Berry or 'the fair young Duchess of Norfolk in shimmering silver lame'. The young brides of wartime had only their meagre handkerchief coupons. No chance of a white wedding for them.

True to form Barbara wrote personally to the Chief Controller and the head of the WAAF. Both replied that they too had raised the matter with the Board of Trade. The Board of Trade – presumably all male – had replied to the effect that 'didn't they know there was a war on?' and that therefore girls could jolly well marry in uniform.

A year later, at a meeting of Welfare Officers in London, she tried again. This time she suggested that if they advertised people might sell their old wedding dresses free of coupons.

The Dowager Lady Loch from West Suffolk had something

to say about this. 'Mrs McCorquodale must have a touching regard for human nature if she thinks she can get people to part with dresses without coupons.'

Many a true word spoken in derision such as that. Mrs McCorquodale *did* have a touching faith in human nature. Still has. And she turned out to be right.

The Lady seemed the obvious place for a wedding-dress advertisement and she duly inserted one. Her reward was two dresses, both, she thought, very pretty. One cost seven pounds, the other eight pounds. They both had their wreath and veil and were so pristine they might have come straight from their maker. She sent both to the Chief Controller with her compliments and the suggestion that others could follow without too much effort. Her offer was accepted and the ATS wedding-dress pool was established.

By the end of the war she had purchased a thousand wedding dresses for the War Office. The drill was that women applied to their Company Commander who arranged for a dress, white, wedding for the use of, to be supplied for one day. Afterwards it was returned in pristine condition ready for the next similarly proportioned ATS bride. The scheme was a huge success and letters of thanks flowed in. Now, in the 1990s, some of those same brides are writing in again as they celebrate their golden wedding anniversaries. They are still grateful that they were able to wed in white.

She also bought forty or fifty for various RAF commands who operated a different system.

'I was limited as to the sum I could give for the dresses,' she wrote subsequently, 'not more than eight pounds, but sometimes I gave a little more out of my own pocket because I understood that those dresses were made of more than satin and tulle, lace and crêpe de Chine; they were made of dreams, and one cannot sell dreams cheaply.'

For a combination of bloody-mindedness and romanticism she has always been hard to beat.

This was not the end of her war effort for she was soon to take on the St John's Ambulance Brigade, an organisation with which she was to remain associated for the rest of her life. It was Edwina Mountbatten's idea. The two women had known each other since the twenties when they were both bright young things, flapping about town with the likes of the Prince of Wales and Lord Louis. In February 1943 Edwina came to stay at Great Barford before speaking to the WAAFs at RAF Cardington.

Shortly before she left Edwina asked Barbara to help with the Brigade's activities in one county. She knew she was doing quite enough voluntary work already, that she had books she should be writing and a young family to bring up. Yet one couldn't say no to the charismatic Edwina who herself did so much too much that it would be shaming to turn her down. So Mrs McCorquodale became the County Cadet Officer. Before long she had recruited more than two thousand boys and girls, often from isolated rural areas or the very poorest areas of towns.

Yet again she demonstrated a highly idiosyncratic verve and ingenuity, irritating the old guard but stimulating the new, writing the words to a new St John's marching song with music by her neighbour Joyce Camden, wife of 'the world-famous bassoonist' Archie Camden.

It begins,

> Knights of St John,
> The White Cross we raise
> Where there's a life to save

and was dedicated to Edwina Mountbatten. According to Dame Barbara the song came to be sung all over the world and was especially popular in Malta and South Africa. The

St John's Ambulance Brigade no longer sing it, much to Dame Barbara's annoyance.

Eventually her work with the Brigade led to her becoming a Dame of Grace of St John of Jerusalem many years before the Queen made her a Dame of the British Empire.

At the end of the war Barbara Cartland was forty-four years old and though she had her daughter and two sons, a husband and her 'wonderful mother Polly' her brothers were gone, as well as a brother-in-law, a first cousin and too many friends to list. She felt that the whole background which she had 'moulded for myself' during the thirties was 'smashed in ruins'.

In 1939 she had been essentially a political animal, her interests 'wholly concentrated on politics'. The death of Ronald took that away from her. At her age she was probably too old to embark on a parliamentary career and yet she was far too energetic and ambitious to settle down and lead the sort of dutiful-wife life that might be expected of a spouse of Hugh McCorquodale – who incidentally had spent much of the war serving with the Home Guard, shooting pigeon for the pot, and generally acting out the part of squirearchical countryman which came most naturally to him.

Despite the camiknickers, the wedding dresses, the libraries, the St John's marching song and much else besides, Barbara Cartland had not even got 'a measly MBE'. The slight rankled. In the years to come she would buckle down and slog away at life until she got her due reward. In the course of the second half of her life she would re-invent herself.

I have spent much time pondering photographs of Barbara Cartland in early life and particularly in the war years both in and out of uniform. In her forties she had poise, a tight perm, tight-lipsticked bee-sting lips, big eyes, slightly hunched shoulders and a general appearance not very much the pretty side of plain. Her uniform may have been made by Worth but it only looks well tailored. See her in civvies, 1945, with Ian and Glen smiling in their sleeveless sweaters and she looks like a demure china doll, indistinguishable from hundreds of other county women who might feature in the pages of 'The Snob Press' – Cartlandspeak for the *Tatler*, *Sketch* and *Bystander*.

Perhaps you can detect a hint of steely resolution about the set of the jaw and the unblinking quality of the eyes, but if you didn't know what had become of her I doubt whether you would find the image of her in the early forties in any way remarkable.

Yet in the second half of her life she was to become unique so that the merest mention of her name was enough to conjure up a vision. A very strange, unexpected, even anachronistic vision.

But a vision none the less.

Chapter Nine

Barbara is middle aged. Raine is 'Deb of the Year' and marries. Barbara turns to very romantic fiction and starts to become seriously famous.

'Y ou will not notice it when you are young,' she wrote in her *Book of Beauty and Health*, 'but look at people over forty who have become hard, unsympathetic and disagreeable. See how it shows in their eyes, in the droop of their lips, in the lines running from nose to mouth and the expression on their faces when they think no one is looking.

'It is quite frightening and whether you are beautiful or ugly in this manner, it is entirely up to you.'

At the end of the war, four years over forty, she was in many ways deeply disillusioned and deprived. It would have been all too easy for her to succumb to self-pity, retreat into herself and become 'hard, unsympathetic and disagreeable'. That, however, was never her style. Her choice therefore was to think positively, pick up the threads of her life and become 'beautiful in this manner'.

But how to do it?

She toyed with the idea of becoming active in politics and was asked to stand in the Conservative interest by two constituency associations. She turned them down, primarily because of her family. Raine was seventeen, Ian eight and

Glen five. She decided she could not be a proper mother to them and a member of parliament too. Nevertheless she spoke every night of the 1945 election campaign, for Alan Lennox-Boyd, Ronald's old friend and her local MP; and for three other candidates. She dined with Beaverbrook; saw Churchill campaigning in the North-East. For those who knew her only in later life as a celebrated romantic novelist in pink, the idea that she might have been a serious political figure is bizarre, yet truly it does seem to have been an option.

She spoke at Lennox-Boyd's eve-of-poll meeting in Leighton Buzzard, which was stormy, with a section of the crowd singing the Red Flag and Mrs Lennox-Boyd being hit over the head with a rolled up copy of *The Times*. Then she and the family retired to Scotland to await the result which came through three weeks later because so many voters were still serving with the forces overseas.

Lennox-Boyd got back; so did Major Gates for whom she had campaigned in Scotland. The other two men for whom she had fought both lost and the crushing Labour victory finally put paid to any thoughts of pursuing a political career, at least for the time being.

She returned to journalism with articles which we would now call 'think-pieces'. One, characteristically, was called 'Let's stop nattering'. Whereas before the war much of her most successful journalism had been social chit-chat of one form or another, she increasingly, as befitted an older wiser woman, turned to venting her opinions in print. In doing so she began to develop a personality and a platform which today's Cartland watchers would recognise instantly and which in essence propounded old-fashioned values though never in an altogether predictable fashion.

This romanticism was to be increasingly echoed in her novels. She was still very far from being a prolific author at this stage in her life. Nor was she best known for her novels. The book which had attracted most attention was probably her biography of Ronald, written during the war, but that was as much to do with the subject as the writing. Winston Churchill himself contributed the preface. She could hardly have expected such an encomium for a work of fiction. Nevertheless she did quite consciously increase her fictional output and whereas in the past she had dabbled in social realism and written about a recognisable world around her, she began deliberately to write romance. Indeed the notion of 'romance' was central to the character she was in the process of inventing.

She was serious too about wanting to devote time and love to her family but at this stage of her life it was one particular member of her family who most preoccupied her: Raine.

Like so many mothers of her generation and social pretensions Barbara had always been obsessive about wanting a son and heir. She has said that 'I don't think I've ever been so thrilled by anything as having a son. I had hoped and prayed for one but everyone had been persistently certain that I was having another girl.'

Perish the thought.

Not only was Raine a girl, she was also the child of that disastrous first marriage. In a sense too she had been the catalyst for the horrible divorce itself for it had been Sachie's threat to take custody of her and remove her from her mother which had been almost as powerful a motive for Barbara issuing proceedings as her husband's adultery itself.

And even though she had become a sort of precocious socialite with numerous gushing write-ups in the 'Snob Press' she was a difficult baby.

When she was six months old in Egypt she collapsed,

went black in the face and was only rescued by Nanny, a bottle of brandy and Barbara's favourite doctor, Sir Louis Knuthsen. Raine was suffering from an enlarged thymus gland. For the first four or so years of her life she only survived 'with the help of fifteen thousand pounds' worth of radium which was strapped to her chest half a dozen times while she slept'. It was said that any sudden shock in those years could have killed her and Barbara was confronted with the choice of bringing her up 'normally' or evacuating her to peace and quiet in the country.

Barbara opted for normality, despite the attendant risks.

'And then a rabbit pops out of a hedge,' she said in justifying her decision, 'and the child dies of shock.'

Raine survived. During the war years she was sent to the fashionable Owlstone Croft School which had been evacuated to a country house near the McCorquodale cottage at Great Barford. Raine was apparently socially embarrassed by the pokiness of the cottage and by the fact that her parents were divorced. Barbara appears to have been a strict mother not averse to judicious corporal punishment, curing her daughter of incipient smoking and drinking by making her smoke a cigarette to the bitter end and drain a filthy cocktail to its dregs. The result is that Raine is a teetotal non-smoker.

It didn't help that Raine achieved good results in her School Certificate. Five distinctions and four credits. On her own admission Barbara was infuriated by this. 'She used to come home at weekends full of her prowess, her prizes and diplomas,' she recalled later. 'She thought I was unkind because I used to say: "Do tidy your hair and clean your face, darling, no man wants a clever woman." ' Raine's gold medal from the London Academy of Music and Dramatic Art was another matter. Talking proper was a prerequisite for a lady.

Actually in the novels Cartland heroines are often extremely bright but Barbara was determined that her daughter should be 'a great beauty'. Nothing else mattered and her immediate goal was the 1947 social season. She was determined that Raine should walk away from it as 'Deb of the Year'. Nothing else would do.

The first step was 'The Monkey Club' or 'Club of the Three Wise Monkeys' an exclusive finishing school in Knightsbridge which was evacuated to Sussex during the war years. As is the practice of such places traditional academic learning was low on the list of priorities but Raine did manage to pursue some serious studies and improved her French and German. Later she went to a Swiss finishing school. Here her French improved still further although Barbara's main motive seems to have been to make sure she got 'decent meals', uncurtailed by Britain's rationing system. Alas Raine reported that the school was doing things on the cheap, fed her on nothing but potatoes and that she had therefore come out in boils. However, she did meet the Hon. Gerald Legge out skiing. He can't have been too put off by the boils because before long he became the first of Raine's three husbands. 'Just like a Barbara Cartland novel,' cooed Barbara, who quite obviously had cast Raine as one of her heroines.

The rest of the family went to Switzerland to visit Raine. Glen hurt himself badly playing on a rocky mountainside. The ever resourceful Barbara was able to take more money abroad than most of her compatriots because she claimed an allowance for a novel based in Switzerland. This was later published as *Wings on My Heart*. With this research allowance she was able to buy some white tulle, yards of blue ribbon and white silk. This would have been unobtainable in England without the requisite coupons. The materials were a vital part in Raine's armoury for the assault on the 1947 'Deb of the Year' title.

She won of course. She was very pretty. Scrupulously neat and tidy. Worth used the Swiss materials to recreate a ball gown of the Empress Eugenie's for Queen Charlotte's Ball. And the result was a foregone conclusion.

The achievement did not necessarily win them friends. The goal was pursued with too much ambition and single-mindedness for that. No less than three dances in her honour – the others given by the Alan Lennox-Boyds and the Sutherlands – seemed excessive. For the dinner party before her own dance Barbara invited twenty-four men. The only women were her mother Polly, Raine and herself. Eight men apiece seemed excessive. 'People were quite shocked,' conceded Barbara, 'as though it was something vaguely immoral to entertain members of the male sex in such undiluted numbers.'

Angela Levin, in her book on Raine and Johnnie, makes it plain that there was at least an ambivalence about Raine, that some thought both mother and daughter excessively pushy and Raine humourless. Some mocked her relative poverty and said she looked good on a shoe-string, others laughed at her enormous crinolines though none as much as the Earl of Dudley who is reported to have asked Raine whether he was supposed to dance inside or outside her dress. Unfortunately Raine's reply is not recorded.

Much of this was almost certainly jealousy. 'Deb of the Year' she was and the following year, though only eighteen, she became bride of the year when she married her mountain-top sweetheart at St Margaret's Westminster where Barbara and Sachie themselves had tied their all-too-flimsy knot some twenty years earlier. The first Barbara knew about the engagement was when she got a telegram in New York where she was visiting American publishers.

Barbara certainly approved of Gerald – later to inherit the earldom of Dartmouth – and speaks kindly of him to this day despite the fact that he is no longer Raine's husband. Whether she approved of the wedding is a moot point. She herself says that she thought Raine too young and inexperienced. Her enemies maintain that she was only too glad to off-load Raine after the expense and bother of her successful London season. Marriage, after all, was the only option for a deb of that period even if she did have five distinctions in School Cert. So if the right man came along why not get on with it?

What is certain, however, is that whereas after both her marriages Barbara remained almost obsessively close to her 'wonderful mother Polly' a distance began to emerge almost immediately between Raine and Barbara. Perhaps Barbara really did resent the fact that Raine had not consulted her over marrying Gerald, much less asked permission. Perhaps Raine did resent her mother's possessiveness and ambition. At all events there was a frisson of froideur which does not always seem to have diminished.

One interesting minor footnote on the subject of dress. At the wedding Raine wore a recycled version of her white coming-out crinoline. The bridegroom's mother, Mrs Humphrey Legge, wore very much what one would have expected of Barbara, pink with a pink-and-grey striped hat. Barbara herself had the sort of hat one might have expected (unkindly described by Angela Levin as looking 'as if it had two mop-heads perched on top'). But the odd thing was that she was dressed entirely in royal blue. Her true pink period was yet to begin.

With Raine's marriage any chance of living out a high-profile public life at second hand was gone. Polly, wonderful Polly, had always lived vicariously. An iron-willed support to her husband and to her children, she was fiercely ambitious for them and championed them ferociously while herself being self-effacing to the point of anonymity. Barbara had enjoyed a certain mild notoriety in the twenties but appeared more than happy to slip into the background when Ronald's success eclipsed her own. Wartime Bedfordshire may have been challenging and entertaining but it was scarcely a world stage. In Raine she had briefly found a champion almost as worthy in her way as Ronald, but now she was gone the only hope of pursuing surrogate fame was through the boys, Ian and Glen. Besotted mother though she was, she must have recognised early that both of them were destined to be solid citizens in the style of the McCorquodales rather than shooting stars like Ronald and Raine.

So if fame and fortune were her goals she would have to achieve them on her own. Her biographer, Gwen Robyns, observes that up until the year of Raine's wedding 'the thirty-five books she had completed were just light-hearted modern love stories'.

This is a myth. I suspect that the myth was fed to Miss Robyns by Barbara herself since the book was authorised and approved. Several of the books she had completed were non-fiction books with serious pretensions, none more so of course than her valedictory biography of Ronald with its preface by Sir Winston Churchill and its foreword by Sir Arthur Bryant. You can say many things about this book but you simply cannot describe it as 'a light-hearted modern love story'. The same is true of *Touch the Stars*, her book on philosophy which the loyal Ronald described as 'a revelation of the person who has shown more courage and virtue in the last two years than most of us can aspire to in a lifetime'.

And even if we accept that her biographer is referring only to the Cartland fiction, how do you explain *Sleeping Swords*, which she finished in 1942? Shortly afterwards she herself said that of the thirty-six novels she had then written, it was the only one she was really proud of. 'Modern' it may be, and it certainly contains a love story, but 'just light-hearted' it most certainly is not.

It is dedicated to Ronald, a sure indication of its seriousness of purpose, for Ronald is, as I think she recognises,
the inspiration of most that is serious about her. Whether she
pulled off a good serious novel is open to debate but that is
certainly what she was intending to do. 'I was so immersed in
politics', she wrote, 'that I felt I wanted the interest and thrill
of them to reach a wider public.' To do this she claims that 'I
think I read every book and pamphlet published during the
period. They were sad fare and one was often ashamed.'

As to whether or not she succeeded, no less than the *Times
Literary Supplement* was enthusiastic. The *TLS* thought she had
been 'clever' in painting a portrait of the century so far, warts
and all and concludes, 'If it were a replica alone, it would
have only a limited interest like most things we have heard
many times over; but there is something new and vigorous,
and strong besides . . . it is difficult to overrate the interest
of these optimistic passages.'

This is high praise in a respectable place and surely gives
the lie to any notion that Barbara Cartland has been a pure
romantic novelist all her life.

This is not the place for detailed literary criticism of
the Cartland *oeuvre*. There is a separate chapter for those
interested in that sort of thing. Suffice it to say, however,
that in 1948 Cartland was a classic example of a moderately
successful author who has not yet found her voice.

That year, spurred on perhaps by the crinolined bride,
the kilted pageboys and the whole romantic aura of Raine's
wedding, a woman's magazine wrote and asked the bride's
mother to write her first historical romance. This was to be
Hazard of Hearts.

Joseph McAleer, in his book on popular culture in Britain
between 1914 and 1950, writes that 'since 1948 every one of
her novels has been set in the period 1790–1914'.

One could argue for ever about the reasons for this and

I rehearse some of the arguments in Chapter Fourteen, but the point here is that in writing *Hazard of Hearts*, Barbara Cartland wrote the first of the many novels with which she has become so firmly identified. Nowadays if you say 'Barbara Cartland novel' you know – or think you know – exactly what to expect.

Henry Cloud, alias John Pearson, in his biography, *Crusader in Pink*, has as accurate a description as any:

> The Cinderella virgin meets and falls in love with her challenging dark hero on the first few pages. Events occur to mar or complicate the course of true love for the next six chapters. But in the seventh, love wins through, the pair are safely married, and we leave them as the joys of licit carnal bliss are just about to start.
>
> But after a lifetime writing just this sort of book, Barbara's skill consists in the endless ingenuity with which she adapts this constant theme to different historical backgrounds and events. Her period extends from the 1790s, when men stopped wearing wigs – 'I never really believe a man in a wig could be an attractive lover,' she explains – until the death-knell of Edwardian England.

Fair enough apart from one rather crucial point. Barbara Cartland had *not*, as Pearson/Cloud supposes, spent 'a lifetime writing just this sort of book'. She never wrote 'this sort of book' until 1948 and *Hazard of Hearts*. She was a mature woman of forty-seven who had been writing novels for a quarter of a century before she suddenly hit on the formula which was to make her world famous.

This was the moment of her second birth.

Chapter Ten

*Barbara and her husband and the boys move
to the country again. She decorates the house
in pink and blue. She is elected to the County
Council. She campaigns for old people and also
for the rights of gypsies.*

After Raine's marriage in 1948 Hugh and Barbara, Ian and Glen, all decided that they wanted to live in the country. All of them had happy memories of the cottage by the Ouse at Great Barford but because of Hugh's work at the family printing business in London 'country' had to be interpreted fairly creatively. Hugh had set his heart on the Hertfordshire green belt thirty or so miles north of London. This was only about an hour's drive from the city but was at least a passable imitation of real countryside complete with shooting, fishing and the essential country pursuits which were so dear to his heart.

The search proved frustrating but eventually they heard that someone called Lord Queenborough had died and that his house, Camfield Place near Hatfield, was consequently up for sale. On a foul, wintry March day the McCorquodales drove north to Camfield and found an enormous pile, 'sad and dilapidated', with walls the colour of dirty margarine and marks where the old pictures had been removed. There was alleged to be a view of private lakes but they were obscured by fog.

Driving away through the gloom Barbara said brightly, if curiously, 'I think I can make it smaller.'

Hugh asked if she was mad. 'I didn't even look,' he said. 'It's impossible.'

It says something about the nature of their relationship that after arguing throughout the weekend they had made a firm decision to put down an offer on Monday. It was accepted and they moved in on 3 May 1950. Barbara has remained ever since and has written more than five hundred books there. It is yet another symbol of her rebirth or re-invention.

Lord Queenborough himself does not seem to have been a wildly significant figure in the history of the house but Barbara soon discovered that Camfield had one really satisfactory literary association. Originally there had been a Tudor house there, indeed there is a famous (and now much exploited) oak tree in the garden which is supposed to have been planted to mark the spot where Queen Elizabeth I shot her first stag. Plausible enough, since as a girl, Elizabeth lived at Hatfield House just round the corner.

In 1867 the Tudor house was razed to the ground by a man called Edmund Potter who had made his fortune as a calico printer and gone on to be Member of Parliament for Carlisle. Potter's house was predictable, exactly the sort of place you would expect of a self-made Victorian seeking to demonstrate his wealth and importance to stuck-up southern neighbours. It is imposingly solid in a style which reminds one of a certain sort of northern town hall.

The grounds and lakes are alleged to be by Capability Brown and Potter seems to have left well alone. They are still lovely.

But the most interesting thing about Edmund Potter is that he had a granddaughter called Beatrix. And Beatrix became the famous author of *The Tales*, a story-teller of a simple, romantic and amazingly popular style which Barbara recognised and to which she was beginning to aspire, albeit in a very different genre. Beatrix had stayed in the house as a child and described it as 'The place I loved best in the world . . . where I have been so happy as a child'. She never forgot 'The note of the stable clock and the all-pervading smell of the new-mown hay, the distant sounds of the farmyard, the feeling of plenty, well assured indolent wealth honourably earned and wisely spent'.

Better still, Barbara believed that Beatrix 'wrote her first book about the rabbits who lived in what we know as the Home Wood'. *The Tale of Peter Rabbit* was set in Barbara's new home.

Magic.

'The locked door in the wall which "the fat little rabbit couldn't squeeze underneath" is exactly the same today without even having been painted!'

The charm of this literary connection had its down-side too. In Margaret Lane's biography of Beatrix Potter there is a description of the little girl sitting in the dining-room with her grandmother and of each one of the six illuminating candles snuffing themselves out one by one. And on the stairs Beatrix described 'two mirrors facing each other on the stairs, miles of looking glasses and little figures in white muslin. I never dare look in them for fear of another head besides my own peeping round the corner.'

Dame Barbara whose religiosity is of a colourful, not to say superstitious, nature, thoroughly believes in ghosts. On the other hand she is naturally robust and took the obvious way out. The rector was summoned to bless the house. Since when it has always had what she describes as 'a happy and peaceful atmosphere'. This is, she stoutly maintains, direct cause and effect.

Renovation and refurbishment took time and money,

though they were limited by legislation which was strictly enforced. The previous year, according to her, someone had been fined twelve thousand pounds and jailed for six months for spending too much money on his house. There was also an extraordinary amount of wall space and a dearth of family pictures. Today, as you walk round the house with Dame Barbara, the numerous middling quality country-house oils seem all of a piece with the fabric of the place. In fact most of them were picked up for a song in the Portobello Road in the early fifties. Even though she has a weakness for gilt and the pink and blue-green of the Pharaohs she has an eye for a bargain and most of the paintings look as if they could have been inherited from the house's predecessor. They fit in.

A year after moving to Hertfordshire she had a hyster-ectomy. The fact that this was almost disastrous was partly her own fault. At first when she was ill vanity led her to refuse to see any doctor until mid-day by which time she was properly made up and had drunk a glass of champagne. She therefore looked and sounded a great deal better than she really was. It was five days before the doctors realised how ill she was. The experience was clearly traumatic. It was also instrumental in concentrating her mind on health in general and on the shortcomings of conventional medicine. This in turn led on to a preoccupation with alternative medicine and eventually to her emergence as a figurehead and spokes-woman for the 'Natural Health' movement. This eventually became almost as crucial a part of her post-menopausal public personality as her romantic fiction. The two fitted together quite plausibly. What could be more obvious than that clean-living romantic heroes and heroines should binge on honey and vitamins? It's where all that sexual energy and clear complexion comes from.

She was keen to continue her work with the St John's Ambulance Brigade, to which she had been introduced by

Edwina Mountbatten during the war. This was good work, of course, and for most of her life she has been keen on good works. It also meant that she was in regular touch with members of the Royal Family. Soon after becoming Vice-President of the St John Cadets in Hertfordshire, for instance, she was one of the organisers of a St John's Exhibition which was formally opened by the Queen, now the Queen Mother, at St James's Palace and subsequently visited by 'many other Royalties'. This was grist to the Cartland mill though there was a snafu at St James's when the doors were shut before the Queen arrived. Barbara was 'absolutely furious' not least because it was all the fault of 'a very bossy woman whom I had tilted with on several occasions'. It takes a bossy woman to know one, let alone tilt at one and the confidence of middle age was making her even bossier than before. This is not to say that she could not flutter her eyelashes, flirt and deploy coquettish feminine charms when the occasion arose but, particularly with other women, she was someone who was not easily thwarted.

Bossy in fact. Sometimes quite rudely bossy, sometimes quite charmingly bossy. Nearly always effectively bossy. But indisputably bossy. Just as she has remained into her nineties.

Not only bossy but busy too. Like her mother she has always had a phobia about boredom and her antidote to boredom has invariably been activity. Even her contemplative pursuits are attacked with a sort of febrile energy. On those idyllic European holidays with Ronald for instance she read books but not in the lazy, languid way that most of us read books on holiday. She devoured them – twenty-one to Ronald's ten. But the most curious aspect of this compulsive activity is that it seems to have increased with age, year by year. As a bright young thing she was energetic, certainly, but not so much more noticeably than anyone else; as a journalist, socialite and political activist, she was filling the unforgiving minute but not so very much more than others of her age and interests. In war she was indefatigable but that was a national characteristic. Now, as she entered her fifties, when most women allow themselves to become matronly, to take afternoon naps, to play bridge and idle away in the wake of their husband's career and wealth, she became more and more hyper-active.

She had been an effective public speaker most of her life and remained so into her nineties: good turn of phrase, attractive deepish voice with very clear if now somewhat archaic diction and apparently boundless self-confidence.

In the early fifties, with Ian and Glen away at prep school and Harrow (where Sachie and Hugh had been together), she was freed from maternal duties except in the school holidays. Yet again one is struck by the apparent contradictions between the advice offered to others and the example she actually set. She has always told other women that their place is in the home looking after their families and yet she seems to have spent much of her life in public, carving out a career, while her children have been entrusted first to nannies and then boarding schools. It doesn't really add up.

Nevertheless this meant that she was free to make a career at a time when less privileged women were making a home and slaving over a hot stove. 'No man who is married should put up with bad food,' she wrote, in a Corgi Mini-Book [sic] called, *Men are Wonderful*. 'No man should permit his wife to say, as so many women do: "Oh, I am not interested in cooking." ' Barbara, as her books on the subject will testify, is passionately interested in diet and in cooking, but that is not quite the same as cooking oneself. Did Hugh allow her to say, 'Oh, I am not interested in cooking'?

So when she was not writing books, or helping to organise the St John's Ambulance, or buying pictures for the house, or penning admonitory articles for the popular press, she was 'already beginning to speak for the Conservative Central Office, for innumerable charities and for other organisations, like the Women's Institutes and the Rotary Clubs'.

In 1953 she published her fiftieth novel. The production of these was beginning to speed up and yet still she had published 'only' fifty novels in the first thirty years of her writing career. In the next forty years she wrote more than five hundred. On my calculation this means that half-way through her life her fiction productivity rose from one and two-thirds books a year to eleven and a quarter a year.

And rising.

In 1955 her political interests and oratorical gifts propelled her for the first time into the realm of elective politics on her own account. When the local Conservatives asked her to stand for the County Council she accepted their offer at the second time of asking. (She pleaded family priorities at first but succumbed when the party came back and said – rather unflatteringly – that they couldn't find anyone else.)

In a way this was unsurprising. Hatfield was already held by Labour – or 'the Socialists', as she still rather quaintly describes them – and the nearby De Havilland factory had just imported a couple of thousand workers to build their new jet-propelled passenger aircraft, the Comet. Barbara and everyone else presumed that nearly all of them would be Labour voters.

Nevertheless she accepted the challenge in just the manner Ronald would have wished. She canvassed seriously, striding down the centre of the street with supporters knocking on the doors to each side of her. If householders expressed no interest she passed on oblivious, but if someone opened the door and showed the slightest curiosity, as well they might seeing the romantic novelist come among them in her pretty hat and sensible shoes, she stopped to talk. She claims to have canvassed eighteen thousand houses and quite apart from the serious political issues, the election generated a huge amount of innocent fun at a time when this was in short supply.

One night Raine, now a London councillor herself and famous for a display of barely controlled fury on discovering unemptied ashtrays and coffee-cups at Heathrow airport, came down to join her mother on a local Brains Trust.

'Britain's most dazzling mother-and-daughter team was doing its stuff' ran one newspaper report under the headline IT'S A KNOCK-OUT WHEN MOTHER MEETS DAUGHTER. Raine, now twenty-six, tripped on, 'ravishing in a sapphire-blue silk dress and a mink wrap she slid off to reveal creamy shoulders. (Murmurs of appreciation).' Her mother, fifty-one, entered sporting 'a plume of electric green feathers on her head and loaded with diamonds. (A stunned silence – biggest compliment a crowd can pay).'

It was hardly the stuff of serious political debate. A typical question was, 'Do our men find foreign girls more attractive than English girls?'

Raine's answer was, 'The trouble is there are too many women to each man – they're getting conceited.'

Barbara's was, 'Foreign girls are getting our men because they're not afraid to say "Darling I think you're wonderful". How many women here have said "Darling, you're wonderful" to their men today?'

This sally was greeted with shrieks of laughter.

Finally, 'Long after the men on the panel had departed, the Magnificent McCorquodales held court in the boilerhouse.

'They talked, laughed, poured drinks for everybody but themselves. They showed no sign of flagging.

'Verdict: They're a pair of knock-outs.'

She won the election against all the odds and remained on the County Council for nine years, mounting some notable and successful campaigns, standing up and being counted, respecting no one much and certainly not the sort of time-serving Captain Mainwaring types who made (and make) up the hard core of local political bodies.

Many years later she said to her friend Jean Rook, the *Daily Express* journalist, that she didn't mind journalists going on about her pills and her pink frocks because nobody sent up Barbara Cartland as effectively as she did herself.

In terms of celebrity and of access to the media the personality which was clearly emerging at the time of the Hatfield election campaign has been an outstanding success. Her cuttings books alone testify to this. Yet Barbara Cartland has never been more than a marginal figure in political terms.

Of course there have been political achievements. Early on in her career as a councillor she visited an old people's home in Hatfield and found seventy-two elderly women crammed into a barely modernised workhouse originally designed for between thirty or forty. Conditions in the home were primitive, the old women were terrorised, the staff were insensitive and Barbara took up the cudgels on their behalf taking as much pleasure, one senses, in pitting herself against the local jobsworths of the Home's Management Committee and the County's Welfare Department as she did in fighting for the rights of these underprivileged and defenceless women.

As a result of her campaign there were improvements to this particular Home. A new kitchen was built, a new sitting-room added, voluntary organisations began to take an interest, a Christmas party was organised with a vast cake and a glass of port for everyone. 'Needless to say', she later wrote with pride, 'the authorities were very angry with me.'

She and Raine were still in cahoots in those days and between them they began to investigate other such Homes around the country. The campaign gathered momentum.

Members of parliament asked questions. Barbara wrote some poignant verses about an old woman who was found dead in bed with a diary in which day after day she recorded the simple message 'Nobody came'. Raine read the poem on Radio Luxembourg.

In March 1956 the Minister of Housing and Local Government, Duncan Sandys, Churchill's son-in-law and an old friend and colleague of Ronald's, instituted a national enquiry into the lot of old people. As a result conditions, allegedly, improved. Barbara is proud to recall that after the parliamentary debate on the matter Sandys sent her the appropriate copies of *Hansard* with a note referring to 'The Gospel according to St Barbara'.

To Gwen Robyns Barbara remarked that she visited every Old People's Home in the county. 'In some I suggested that a little Jeyes' Fluid might be a good thing.'

The other political campaign of which she is proudest is the one she fought on behalf of the local gypsies. As 'Romanies', gypsies might seem an entirely appropriate cause for Britain's most prolific romantic novelist, though many people in Britain regard them as being far from romantic.

The Cartland view was actually not particularly starry eyed. Indeed it was almost pragmatic. It was the practice in the early nineteen-sixties to move gypsies on every twenty-four hours. Barbara's case, as expressed at an official enquiry in February 1963, was that 'Everyone agrees it is unjust and unfair that people should be denied education when they ask for it . . . but how can you educate children who must move on every twenty-four hours?'

Like all Cartland campaigns it had rumbustious moments, poignant moments, and frankly ludicrous moments. *The Times* report that 'a gas cylinder, a milk churn, a dustbin and a perambulator . . . are not litter within the meaning of the act' is a judgement worthy of the presiding justice in N.F. Simpson's *One Way Pendulum*. In 1960 an impecunious Romany called Israel Buckland was fined three pounds by the local magistrates for 'illegal camping'. Barbara paid the fine for him – a splendidly romantic gesture and one which was gratifyingly certain to infuriate the hated 'authorities'.

She originally became involved with the gypsies in her capacity as President of the Hertfordshire Branch of the Royal College of Midwives. One of her Hertfordshire midwives was involved with a pregnant gypsy mother whose caravan near Hatfield was being moved on every twenty-four hours. The pregnant mother was supposed to have the baby at St Albans hospital and she also had an eight-year-old daughter who should have been receiving regular schooling. The midwife was upset by what she felt was the persecution of her charge and complained to Barbara.

Barbara sensed outrage and Pecksniffery at once. Being a County Councillor she at first played it by the book and raised the matter at the next council meeting. She might as well not have bothered. In Gwen Robyns's succinct words 'she learnt that nothing was being done'.

Doing nothing is simply not in her character. Speedily and with gusto, she caused something to be done.

John Pearson called his pseudonymous biography *Crusader in Pink*. The title conjures up a vision of the Dame buckling on a diaphanous tutu which is not wholly removed from the truth. She *is* a doughty fighter; she *is* courageous; she has no respect for authority. But would you really want her on your side? When it comes to causes, too, is her judgement entirely sound? Camiknickers and gypsies? Wedding dresses and subsidies for the working mum? Try as you may, love her as, in the end kicking and protesting I think all who know her do, you have to concede that in everything she does she is to an extent a player in the theatre of the absurd.

In the end, however, it really doesn't matter. You cannot help but admire her courage and her energy.

In the autumn of 1993, when she was ninety-two years old, she sent me a letter which had been printed in the *Welwyn and Hatfield Times*.

Sir,
   The recent story of the baby of two left at home alone every day for two years is appalling. It makes me more convinced than I am already that the idea I put forward to every member of the House of Commons in June 1991, is the only way to treat our children in the future.
   I suggested that the mother should not receive Child Benefit as they do now but *be paid* to stay at home for the first five years of the child's life so that it has the love and attention of its Mother.

What, I wonder, would Dame Barbara's reaction have been if the state had paid *her* to stay at home for the first five years of her children's lives? Shock, horror, outrage and almost certainly a campaign to allow young mothers the freedom to do as they wish. Yet again conventional consistency is simply not her style.

She continued.

We all know now this would prevent the crimes which are committed every day by unwanted children who have never known love and affection.
   The members of parliament were not impressed and merely said that they would increase the Child Benefit in the autumn which was not the right answer.
   In the meantime, after I had started this campaign, France brought it in and so did Sweden.
   Today's appalling story follows the endless horrors which take place when the children are taken 'Into Care'.
   I can only beg those who are really worried about the Future Generation, to think again about this very simple

way of making a child happy, contented and properly looked after. At least for the first five years of its life.

Her signature is appended. You can argue the case any way you wish. You can certainly, as so often with Dame Barbara, question the consistency and ask about sauces for geese and sauces for ganders. But what the editor of the *Welwyn and Hatfield Times* and you, gentle reader, did not get, was the Dame's covering letter.

It was very brief. It said, simply, 'This is my present fight, Love Barbara.'

Chapter Eleven

I am invited to luncheon. It is very creamy. Dame Barbara talks on the sofa about marriage and Claridge's and the Duke of Windsor and blue blood and her white Rolls Royce.

U sually when I went to Camfield Place I was invited for tea. Afternoon tea at table is Dame Barbara's preferred entertainment, at least during the week. It comes around four o'clock when she has recovered from reciting the latest several thousand words of novel while reclining on the *chaise-longue* in the library. She wields the heavy tea-pot with unshaking hands, feeds the labrador and the Pekinese on cake, insists you have some yourself, as well as delicate crustless cucumber sandwiches, miniature meringues and scones and all the other traditional paraphernalia associated with honey and the Grantchester church clock but which scarcely exists outside such post-Imperial time warps as the Empress Hotel, Victoria or the Peninsula Hong Kong.

One September day in 1993, however, I was bidden to luncheon.

Dame Barbara and Nigel her long-serving cook had pushed out the boat. There was a half bottle of champagne in a bucket, exclusively for me since she no longer drinks alcohol at lunch. As an hors d'oeuvre Nigel had made one of his specialities, a tomato stuffed with a whole egg and cream;

then there was a delicious kouliabac, with cream and salmon kedgeree mixture encased in a shiny fish-shaped pastry crust each scale lovingly sculpted; then a vacherin with meringue and cream and strawberries followed by an inspired cheeseboard including a creamy new discovery from France.

Afterwards I even had a glass of port and I am not ashamed to say that by late afternoon back in London I felt replete to the point of biliousness. It was delicious, all of it, yet rich beyond belief. What struck me as most extraordinary, however, was that although she drank no alcohol Dame Barbara, at ninety-two, managed to eat as much as I did without any ill effect whatever. At ninety-two her stamina extended even to gastronomy. Cholesterol seemed to mean nothing and I could only suppose that, iron constitution apart, it must have something to do with all those pills.

I arrived at half past twelve and left shortly before five and in the whole of that time Dame Barbara scarcely ceased from talk.

I have tried, in this book, to convey something of her history and something of her flavour and character, to tell her as she is and was, to put her into context, and do all the things that a biographer is supposed to do with those he biographises, but you will never have the woman quite right if you do not listen to her talk a little as she is apt to do on that sofa in the drawing-room surrounded by the bowls and vases of pink flowers with the bow window looking out across the grass lit by autumn sunlight to the lake where Max Hastings, Editor of the *Daily Telegraph*, once shot her favourite duck. (She believes he did it on purpose. He denies it. Their two accounts of the incident are alarmingly divergent!)

Hers is a voice out of time, a stream of consciousness as brilliant and eclectic as anything contrived by the great stage monologuists like Barry Humphries, Frankie Howerd or Ken Campbell.

To be sure it is raw material, the bricks from which to construct an edifice. Even so if you don't catch a few minutes of the Dame in flight you cannot really understand. Here she is then, aged ninety-two, after that heavy, delicious, creamy lunch. I have edited out one or two of the more risqué and libellous stories and I have not included my side of the conversation. Had I done so it would have covered no more than a quarter of a page and would have consisted of very little more than the occasional 'Ah, but . . .' or 'Surely . . .'. For when she pauses Dame Barbara does so only so that she can draw breath, not so that anybody else can articulate more than a very few words.

As Libby Purves once said of her in *The Times*, 'Sorry. This is not an interview. You don't do interviews with forces of nature.'

She was sitting on the sofa, talking about men, marriage and Mountbatten with tremendous verve and relish, hands pumping the air, eyes flashing, every phrase punctuated with a breeze of a chuckle, every paragraph with a gale of laughter.

'You've got to be very careful of love. As I say, he was frightfully attractive and he loved me very much. I've got masses and masses of letters from him all saying, you know, how much he loved me. But the point was, it would have been a mistake. First we couldn't afford to get married. Secondly I've got a great friend who's the Duke of something, oh what's his name, you know the name, quite well. Well he's been hounding her to marry him. She's got a large family and a house just like this. Large family, and he's a Duke.

'Darling, the day he dies . . . out. So she said, "What's going to happen to our families?" And he said, "Please marry me, please marry me." He says that every day. She says she doesn't see how she can. I mean, don't you see, nobody today lives in *two* enormous houses. She's not going to live in *his* house and the moment he's dead the next of kin moves in. And she can't keep *her* house up with him and her large family – they're all devoted to her, she's awfully nice, coming in and out, you know, if she's not there. So what do you do? She lets the Duke kneel every day. That's all.

'Now you do see it is a problem when people are old. You do see it's a frightful problem. If it doesn't work, then where are you? You see? You've got to be very careful. . . .

'Now think what else we ought to think of now . . .'

A very brief pause while I ask a question. She sort of half hears it, isn't tremendously interested, but then picks up on the word 'Claridge's'. This triggers a response.

'I went to Claridge's you see first in 1919. It's in the books. It was the first day I'd been to Church Parade and twenty-five per cent was horse drawn. The Dorchester wasn't there then. Do you realise that? It wasn't there till 1927. So you sat looking at that very nice garden and that lovely house. And the man who owned it was Lord, oh, what's his name, I'll think of it in a moment, he's Glen's godfather. When I had a divorce and had nowhere to go for the moment because they made it, er, difficult, and pretended the furniture was theirs, so I went to stay at the Dorchester because Lord, I'll think of his name in a moment, he only ever went to bed with countesses, no duchesses, he always went to bed with duchesses. He arranged that I should have a room at the Dorchester. Think now. With a bathroom. One of those ones with windows. Pound a night. I stayed there three months at a pound a night.

'Then the Cunningham-Reids said to me, remember people were wonderful to me, they thought I'd been done down, people always love it when you've been done down, anyway they said any minute you're not asked out by a young man – though, of course I was always out with young men – come to us, there's always a meal for you here. So you never had to have a meal. Mary was my greatest friend and I did spend a lot of time with her but there we were.

'I must say, it was rather amusing the other day, they asked me to be on this thing which is going to be the great film of the year which is er the House of Windsor. And I tried to tell stories. I hope I haven't overdone it. Of different people, d'you see. Because, of course, I've known what was her name, who married the Prince of Wales, you see I'm tired today, come on you know the woman who broke up, Wallis Simpson. Well I'd known Simpson you see ever since I was seventeen. It's in the book, you've got it there. He tried to kiss me which I thought was a good story. I really told the story about her and how she was very plain.

'And then I told this one which I thought was really rather good. They'll cut it out of course because they were here for three hours. You know they've got ten million people. If I get three minutes I shall be very surprised. The story I told which was quite amusing was that I went on my honeymoon and as I went into Maxims there were those two on *their* honeymoon. He went off to the gentlemen's and she was there and so I thought shall I curtsey or shall I not curtsey? I asked Edwina what she was going to do and Edwina said well if it makes him happy, what's it matter. I curtsey to anyone if it makes them happy. So I gave her a bob d'you see. And then I said hello and she said I hope you'll be as happy as we are. But apparently – which I couldn't put in but which is frightfully funny – my husband, who didn't speak French went into the gentlemen's and a man said "*non, non, monsieur*", but he paid no attention and said "Oh, out of the way" and there was the Prince in there, and of course he knew him so they had a long talk and when they came out I curtsied and we went in to dinner and I was at a middle table and they were on a sofa at the side with a lot of friends and they were all talking when suddenly the Prince said "I want some butter ... butter, waiter! ... butter, waiter!" All in English. Darling, nobody paid the slightest attention. I thought, Oh how sad! You see. I was trying to think of amusing stories for each of the people. It breaks it up.

'Now what else did I say ... I went on for hours. Three hours. Too long. I'll show you the twenty-six questions they asked. They sent me the questions, all of which, well I inched round them, most of them, you see, because they were terribly boring and you didn't want to answer them. Anyhow, oh I mustn't criticise and the one thing is we must keep the royalty. They're so badly advised. Dame Barbara then told a story which, by the standards of the time, was innocuous to a degree. One hears infinitely more malicious tittle-tattle about the Royal Family every day in public and in private. Nevertheless, Dame Barbara is very sensitive to the charge that she has in any way exploited her relationship with the Royal Family and in deference to her wishes I have put a blue pencil through this particular anecdote. She herself agonises, publicly and privately, about the plight of the House of Windsor, but she does not wish, understandably, to be seen to be rocking the royal boat.

'I told the story again, I told it this morning, I told it you before, about the man from Australia and the King of Greece. He didn't know, he hadn't heard of it. Well if he hadn't heard of it ... You see they've got nobody there now. They haven't got a soul you see. They had Dickie and Dickie was wonderful and Dickie told me all the news. But I didn't *know* them and you never put "you" in the letters. Frightfully difficult I can tell you to write a letter. You put "Your Majesty" every half second and it's a bloody nuisance. The Queen Mother sent me *such* a nice telegram because I sent her a present again. How much do you think he left? You know, her comptroller, who we all loved. Martin Gilliatt. Did you see? Million and a half. And he sent me just the other day, two hundred and fifty pounds for St John's and I thought perhaps he was depriving himself and I was so worried about him and thinking he'd sent too much, do you know. One million and a half. Can you believe it? Where did he get it from? He lived somewhere down here. Everyone loved him, he always said nice things and I loved him very much but I never thought of him as being important or having money except that he was Comptroller of the Queen, the Queen Mother. Most of them haven't got sixpence have they? Million and a half. He left two million but some of it had to go in a peculiar way. I tell you things are always surprising you. You don't expect it.

'Now what else are you putting in? What you really ought to do is go through all the press cuttings in there. Glenny's done them all for me and he's only put in the nice things because he said Dickie would never put in anything nasty about himself. And there are all the letters. All the royal letters but I don't *think* we can use them. You see that really *is* rather dreadful. You see the Prince of Wales behaved so badly. Not this one. The old Prince of Wales. Now I wrote to him. I knew him very well and I said, look the man who always used to serve you at the Embassy Club is . . . oh it was his fiftieth birthday or he was giving up or something. And I said, "will you drop him a line?" And he wrote me back in his own hand saying, "You tell him that I wish him good luck." Well it wouldn't have hurt him to have written himself and then the man could have kept the letter for ever. But nobody ever told him at home. That's what's so bad. They ought to be told. It wouldn't have hurt him. He was very, very bad like that. Always was. A lot of it was, of course, because his father didn't like him. I've said very little about his father but he was always finding fault because, oh, remember they had big trousers. He said he was overdressed.

I remember when I'd done the Embassy up, he was one of the first people who came in wearing a dinner jacket. It had only just been invented by what was that very nice man who was a friend of mine, he was on the stage. He invented it and the Prince of Wales wore it. Everyone was horrified because everyone was in a white tie and tails. It's awfully difficult to make them understand today that people dressed up. When you think of the sloppy way that girls today . . . I mean you should see my granddaughters . . . they're *appalling*, in trousers, you know, which don't fit . . . men's breeches . . . and, oh God, their faces are un-made-up, their hair all hanging about . . . terrible. I'm hardly surprised people won't marry them. I wouldn't marry them. It's extraordinary that it's changed so much.

'It changed when women started to be so pushy. "I must be a man. I must go and fight in the war" and all this rubbish. What do they expect to happen if they put twenty women on a ship which is going away for several months? And, you see, what is so wrong is that now everybody wants to find something wrong.

'Oh and do put in the story about how Raine met Princess Elizabeth. Don't you think that's always a good story? Saying what a pretty little baby and what a funny name. Why did I christen Raine, Raine? Well it had to be a single name because of McCorquodale. That's why I called one son Ian and the other Glen. And it *is* a Gaelic name. And I wasn't so certain then as I am now that I was so, er, grand. Did you read the new thing? I've found out that I've got blue blood from the Hamiltons too. Did you see that?

'In 1972 I said I'll have a Rolls that'll last me my lifetime. It cost nine hundred pounds. So they said what colour would you like? And I said I'll have a white. "White?" they said, because, d'you know, no white cars. People would stop dead

Barbara with her famous eponymous glider.
This was one of her earliest campaigns
but it was only during the war that she was proved right.

Barbara the campaigner: health and beauty, the proper labelling of food, gypsies, and much else besides.

Barbara and bed: her own four poster at Camfield Place.
(Bed is where her hero and heroine always end up, but never on the printed page.)

The archetypal Cartland couple
pirouetting in Selfridge's shop window
as their creator looks on.

Barbara and a bevy of celebrities: Gloria Swanson; Diana Dors and husband; Dr Coggan, the Archbishop of Canterbury. She has been collecting celebrities for over ninety years and has even written a book about them.

Barbara's latest Christmas card:
'Greetings and Love from Barbara'.

in the street to photograph it. Everything's a white car now. No white cars in England in those days. And they'd never made a white Rolls before. There were no white cars about. Now everything's white. Quite right too. You can see them. People stopped in Bond Street and said "Can we photograph you?" It was absolute pandemonium having one. Needless to say it didn't last. Fell to bits. I wrote to the chairman who I didn't know and I said "your car's fallen to bits". And he said "Oh. Well perhaps you can bring it in to Crewe and have it pass its MOT and we'll see what we can do." So I sold it to a man who's using it as a punkah for weddings and . . . what a surprise . . . he didn't want to part with . . . well, when I took it d'you see, I said to the boys, um, can I have a number and they said "*really!* What do you think you are? Only tarts have a special number." Well I said, "Royalty has a special number" so I said I'm going to have a special number, so they had to give me one and it cost five hundred pounds so my husband, well he was dead anyway, and so I had his favourite number which was twenty-nine, BC twenty-nine, d'you see?

'*Now* . . . um, the man who's bought it has got BC, so don't tell me he's not claiming it's from my car. He wouldn't give me tuppence farthing for it so I got it back from him and he's got BC a hundred and seven.

'And you'll have to put Raine in, marrying this new man. And I rang the Lord Lyon and he was awfully sweet and I said to him, look am I really allowed to say that my grandmother was the direct descendant of Robert the Bruce? He said "yes". So I said "Can I say I am?" And he said "of course". So I said "Are you quite sure because you know people will say I'm pushing" and he roared with laughter and said "It's quite all right. Tell them to come to me. And yes you are." So there you are. So I'm delighted. I've got a king on one side. And I've looked up the Hamiltons. And

I've found that the fifth earl or something married Princess Margaret of England who was the widow of one of the kings. So I've got royal blood both sides. I tell you why I was doing it. Not really for myself but because I use it in my books.

'I do so much of when the Queen was sending people to save people in the Balkans by having an English Queen you see. She ran out of Queens so in my book I have to find a new one. There are Scottish ones of course. The Stuarts had six Kings of Scotland but they weren't acknowledged by the British. The only one who was was Robert the Bruce. He only had two years, poor darling, and then he died. Rather interesting. Anyhow I've become thoroughly Scot now. They're so nice to me in Scotland. The English are so rude and disagreeable and tiresome and have such bad manners. I'm fed up with them. I did wear tartan in Scotland but I don't bother now. I've got my son properly tartanned out. Would you believe the McCorquodales haven't worn it for a hundred years. They never bothered. And they wore, for no reason at all that I can imagine, the Black Watch trousers. So I wrote to the Lord Lyon and he wrote back and said "yes, it hasn't been done for a hundred years . . ." I want you to see the house. Outside the gentlemen's loo which you must look at because it's full of things, is the family tree going right back to the Duke of whatever he was. I'll think of it in a moment. I'm terribly tired today. And he was a pagan. And he conquered Norway. He had three kings – Ethelred the Unready, Ethel . . . oh whatever he was . . . and King Canute. They were his grandsons and his great-grandson was William the Conqueror.'

And then we were on our feet, tripping off to look at four-poster beds and family portraits and a dressing-room stacked with pink sequinned ball gowns. Nevertheless the monologue barely faltered.

Every time I visited her she talked like that. From such

outpourings you can, of course, extrapolate, distil, deduce and generally construct. But I have never known anyone else talk like her and I make no apology therefore for taking a loop of Cartland at speed on the sofa and reproducing it virtually verbatim.

Only then will you believe.

Chapter Twelve

*Her son Ian is in charge of 'Cartland Pro-
motions'. He promotes his mother. She has
fallen out with several publishers. Her books
are sold with butchers' meat. Ian invents a
special Barbara Cartland Romance Club. Ian
says his mother's books have sold six hundred
million copies. Foreigners love her very much.*

The headquarters of Cartland Promotions is in a distinctly dingy office at the back of a dilapidated mews building in London's Pentonville Road. Camfield Place is the word factory and the Dame's Literary Agent is Rupert Crew, a cover name for two lady agents who have looked after the sale of Cartland books for years but who do not loom very large in the scheme of things. 'I control them,' says Dame Barbara's elder son, Ian, a touch ominously. In other words, these remorselessly unromantic premises are operational HQ.

Ian is one of three partners in Cartland Promotions along with his mother and his brother Glen. (Glen, amazingly for a member of this family, is shy of publicity and does not like to talk to the press if he can possibly avoid it.) Glen is a relatively sleeping partner; Mother is, in effect, the product; Ian is Managing Director.

To reach the actual Cartland office you have to negotiate a seriously dilapidated driveway and staircase both apparently deserted. When you do get there the office is marginally more luxurious but not a lot. It was late March when I first went there and the secretary was still wearing an overcoat. The staff appears to be her and Barbara's son Ian. It does not feel like the hub of a great business empire.

Ian was on the telephone. The bare facts about Ian may be gleaned from *Debrett's People of Today* and since he is chairman of *Debrett's* there is a reasonable chance that these bare facts will be accurate as far as they go.

> Son of Hugh McCorquodale (MC) and Dame Barbara Cartland DBE (qv); bro of Countess Spencer qv; b 11 Oct 1937. Educ. Harrow, Magdalene Coll Cambridge; m Anna, née Chisholm; 2 da; career former commercial and export manager British Printing Corporation; chm Debrett's Peerage Ltd., Media Investments Ltd., partner Cartland Promotions 1976–; dir Royal Exchange Art gallery; Recreations fishing, shooting, gardening, tennis. Clubs Boodles, Whites; Style – Ian McCorquodale Esq., 111 Whitehall Court, London, s.w.1.

Points to note from this bald resumé of a life and times are as follows:

Ian is a moderately public figure but exists in the popular imagination largely as 'son of Barbara' and 'brother of Raine'. Thus when, in August 1993, the *Daily Telegraph* city pages announced that he had joined the board of a new conglomerate the story was headed CARTLAND BOY WITH PLENTY OF NOVEL IDEAS. When, that same year, *Hello!* wrote him up in a four-page feature, the article was headed 'Barbara Cartland's eldest son talks about his mother and sister Raine'. Nevertheless it is worth noting that whereas Barbara's entry in *Who's Who* is the longest of all and includes every single one of her book titles, her entry in Ian's book, *Debrett's People of Today* is comparatively modest and runs to a mere thirteen lines.

'Anna, née Chisholm' and he are, sadly, no longer married but this has left him more time to be with 'Mum'. He, like Glen, now goes down to Camfield practically every weekend. The reference to his career with the British Printing Corporation is based on the fact that the family firm was taken over by BPC and Ian ultimately left to carve out a career on his own, principally as the driving force behind Cartland Promotions. Despite his genial exterior Ian, when it comes to business, is a relative whizz. Colin Draper, the former chief executive of Thomas Tilling who recruited him to the board of his new conglomerate in 1993, said of him, 'he has a wide range of very useful business contacts. He is a good, solid citizen, well recognised in the City.' A safe pair of hands, in other words, though I suspect this is to underestimate him.

When I called in one morning he was at his desk beaming and doodling in a dark-grey pin-stripe suit. He reminded me, in that improbable Islington office, of a character in an early *Avengers* episode. The tea came in a cup decorated with Cartland pink roses. The secretary serving it was still in her overcoat. It *was* very cold. We appeared to be the only people in the entire building. It was all oddly surreal.

'Have you not sold the videos on to Japan yet?' he was enquiring into the telephone. He has the endearing, old-fashioned English quality of seeming to think that on balance the whole thing, life itself, is a bit of a lark. 'A bit like *The Darling Buds of May* sort of thing', he continues, 'but more upmarket . . . I'll have to think this one through; then I'll have a word with Mum about it.' A word with Mum is crucial and continual. Often, in the drawing-room at Camfield Place, a call comes through from Ian and words are exchanged. They do not always seem as cosy as one might expect between the great romantic novelist and the son on whom she dotes. 'We're too alike,' says Ian. They love each other dearly but they do spat.

'Let me have a word with Mum,' said Ian again, adding as a final thought, 'he'd pay a royalty on it, presumably?'

He presumably would. This is nothing if not a commercial enterprise.

Nevertheless the whole business of Dame Barbara's success is a little perplexing. When I first started hawking the idea of writing about her to British publishers I was met with considerable scepticism. The *on dit* in British publishing was that the books simply did not sell. If they did sell in large quantities then why did she write quite so many? As a very general rule publishers do not like their authors, including their best-sellers, to produce more than one book a year. If a best-seller is more prolific than that they will almost always take on a pseudonym. Thus writers such as P.D. James or John le Carré never produce more than one novel a year. And when someone such as Ruth Rendell feels compelled to write two a year she does the second under another name, Barbara Vine.

In her nineties, however, Barbara Cartland was, if anything, accelerating. A novel a fortnight flies in the face of all conventional publishing wisdom. Moreover if each one was selling as well as the Dame and Ian imply then there simply wouldn't be the need to produce quite so many. In 1992 she had written to me, 'The British are hopeless in selling books.' For 'books', read '*my* books'.

In the beginning, of course, she was, as a novelist, much less frantic. My calculation is that she wrote a mere seven novels in the first ten years of her career as against an average of twenty or more a year in her eighties and nineties. In terms of stamina, geriatric creativity and sheer bloody-mindedness this achievement deserves its place in the *Guinness Book of Records*. In terms of effectively making money it is, to put it mildly, unorthodox.

Gwen Robyns claims that her very first book, *Jigsaw*, made two hundred and fifty pounds, went into six editions and was translated into five languages. The book, like other early Cartlands, was published by George Duckworth but when I asked Colin Haycraft, the present boss of the company, for corroboration he had to reply that 'In spite of diligent search I can find nothing in the files appertaining to this author'.

For many years after Duckworth, Barbara Cartland novels were published by Hutchinson, now absorbed into the Random Century Group. This came to an end in 1984. Ian's version is that Hutchinson 'faded out of the scene as sales declined'. The *Times* Diary of the day had a starker story which suggested mutual bitterness and acrimony. Dame Barbara was quoted, memorably, as saying of Hutchinson, 'They are such disagreeable people, and they've no manners at all.'

Not so, according to Paul Sidey, who used to be her editor: 'The manner of her "sacking" was grossly misreported by that journalist on the *Times* Diary,' says Sidey. 'It taught me a lesson. Only do puffs. Until his piece, there was no acrimony, merely the decision not to continue publishing in Hutchinson and Arrow as a result of generally declining sales. I wrote to Barbara afterwards to apologise most sincerely for the Diary piece. And that was the end of it.'

The relationship with her editor and publishers at Hutchinson was cordial but oddly distant.

'We never met,' says Sidey. 'Proofs were picked up by her chauffeur from the Savoy, and she didn't like to be edited – even for her punctuation, use of capital letters, or blurbs (which she supplied).

'Over the telephone we remained on perfectly good terms, and she once gave me some very good advice on some pills to counteract Montezuma's Revenge in Mexico: "They're only tiny, dear, but they bind like concrete." '

Tony Whittome was an editor at Hutchinson during those halcyon days in the sixties and seventies when Barbara Cartland novels were selling fabulously. Indeed it is not unduly fanciful, he thinks, to claim that in those years

Barbara, with a little help from Denis Wheatley, practically kept the company afloat.

Whittome says that Barbara's editor in those days was Dorothy Tomlinson, who was small but 'formidable and fiery'. If Barbara was the Queen of Romance, Dorothy was the Queen of Romantic Editors. She was paramount and had a full hand of Queens of Romance as her authors, all of them fiercely jealous of each other. So jealous, in fact, that it was Hutchinson policy to keep them apart and try to ensure that in the office they never met.

On one legendary occasion, however, something went wrong and Barbara and one of the other Queens – it might have been Ursula Bloom, it might have been Denise Robins – found themselves at opposite ends of a long corridor converging on Dorothy's office, half-way along it.

For a second the two Queens froze like gunmen in a Gary Cooper Western; then simultaneously they both managed a quavering cry of 'Daaahling!' before clutching each other in a frozen embrace. The incident lived on in Hutchinson folklore but was never repeated.

Whittome says that though he never had much to do with Barbara personally he observed the performance and marvelled at its star quality. She really came into her own at the sales conference. 'She cared much more about the reps than the editors,' says Whittome drily, 'which showed sound judgement.' She would sweep up in the white Rolls Royce and flatter them all outrageously. On one occasion she even gave each rep a phial of some miraculous elixir guaranteed to enhance their virility, potency and all-round energy, thus enabling them to sell even more of her books than usual in the impending campaign.

Since Hutchinson bowed out of her life her UK publishers became Mandarin and Severn House. Mandarin publish fourteen titles a year in paperback and Severn

House a further two. Since she is presently writing more than twenty a year, production is exceeding publishing capacity by at least four books a year! Sales, according to Ian, average between twelve to fifteen thousand copies per title. He says that publishers consider this 'reasonably good bread-and-butter publishing in today's market'. He adds with a touch of bitterness that 'the publishers do nothing in the way of promotion or advertising of the books'.

Publishers' sales figures are always a minefield of misinformation but twelve to fifteen thousand copies per title in paperback only certainly does not put the Dame into the best-seller category.

Ian does not have a publishing background so he is not wedded to the traditional conservative ways of the British Book Trade. At the very beginning of his association with Barbara Cartland Promotions he hit on the idea of selling 'part books' instead of 'part works'. Sales were made through newsagents rather than bookshops and at the end of the exercise forty hardback titles of 'The Latest and Greatest Barbara Cartlands' had sold more than seven hundred and fifty thousand copies at £1.95 each.

In another unorthodox campaign Ian joined forces with Dewhurst the butchers. Every time someone bought more than twelve pounds' worth of meat from Dewhurst they got a 'free' Barbara Cartland novel. Each one was individually shrink-wrapped to stop it getting covered in blood.

Not for the first time I feel there is something contrary going on here, that there is something inconsistent in the honey-loving, natural-vitamin health freak becoming involved in a scheme to turn us all into carnivores. Nevertheless by the time this promotion was over three hundred and fifty thousand Cartlands had been given away and Dewhurst's share of the market increased by four per cent despite the fact that this was a difficult period for meat sales due largely to the unseasonably hot summer of 1989!

Ian's latest brainchild is the Barbara Cartland Romance Club, launched to an astonished world at Camfield Place early in October 1993. A breathless Libby Purves who reported the event for *The Times* wrote that: 'For a mere £9.95 a month her fans get two hardback novels, a cassette, an oak leaf and a newsletter on how to make your husband happy.' Ms Purves wrote a funny article about the event and was plainly captivated by the Dame.

Listening to the Dame discuss the seating plan (how furious some people would have been to hear them being relegated to positions below the salt!) I was struck as usual by her ebullient, no-frills, common sense. The club was another of Ian's bright ideas; she was mildly sceptical; but why not? If it generated income, she'd do it. She needed the cash. Raine apparently is always chiding her for self-promotion such as this and for talking to journalists. This makes Dame Barbara snappish. If she didn't do such things she would be thousands of pounds the poorer. It's all very well for Raine . . .

Nevertheless she is, in the United Kingdom, no longer a best-seller in the accepted sense. Her cumulative sales over the years must be enormous but it takes all Ian's guile and ingenuity, and all her own energy and charisma, to shift copies to her fellow countrymen. She is a phenomenon all right, arguably the best-known writer in the country and indeed, in Libby Purves's words 'a force of nature'. But she is not, on home turf, an authentic best-seller.

However, the United Kingdom market is a relatively unimportant one for the author lucky enough to have English as his or her mother tongue. The real gold-mine is the United States.

I was surprised to discover that Dame Barbara did not have a single book published in the United States until she was an old age pensioner. That was in 1967, the year she completed her hundred and fourteenth book.

Both Barbara and Ian maintain that the reason for her sudden late-flowering popularity both in the States and elsewhere has been due to the growth of pornography and later to the AIDS epidemic. The lore, according to Cartland Promotions, is that other 'romantic' novelists sold out to the pornographic trend but only Dame Barbara persevered with 'a pure type of romance, with a chaste heroine and a happy ending which is never complete without the couple being married during the last chapter'.

When I looked at the texts carefully I was less than certain that this is quite right. On the other hand the Cartland publicity machine is persuasive. 'People are tired of sex, sex, sex, until it's beastly and unpleasant' reported Libby Purves in her *Times* article about the launch of the Cartland club, 'More love. You media are so powerful – say yes, yes, yes to the good things not the bad.'

This was the sort of message a significant Middle-American readership was evidently avid for in the late sixties and early seventies. Pyramid published her at first, with some success, but in 1973 they were succeeded by Bantam who published two titles a month. At one stage sales were exceeding four hundred thousand copies per title. This really did put her in the best-seller league. After a whirlwind tour of the States in 1976 with a series of live TV appearances ('Everyone except Johnny Carson,' says Ian), she found herself at number one and two in the *Dalton Weekly* best-seller list. This feat remains, according to Ian, unequalled before or since.

Bantam gave way to Berkeley in 1982 and since then have been producing one a month. These sell approximately forty thousand per title and after a dip sales are once more increasing. To date her total American sales are one hundred and fifty million.

This is about five times her total French sales but France is a buoyant market and both Ian and the Dame take a perverse but proper pride in the notion that an Englishwoman in her nineties can take on the French at what is popularly perceived to be their own game and come out on top. J'ai lu, her French publishers, were publishing two new titles and two reissues every month. Total sales were running at an estimated million a year, helped by pegging the cover price of each book to a mere 18 francs.

In Germany she had four different publishers producing thirty new titles a year till 1993 when one dropped out and the figure fell to twenty new titles a year. Scandinavia has twelve new Cartlands a year in addition to a Danish magazine which contains a complete book in each of ten annual issues selling fifteen thousand copies a time. The Spanish have been publishing two titles a month at ten thousand copies a time for some time; the Italians are just beginning. Greece is in the pipeline.

The latest growth area is Eastern Europe and the former Soviet bloc. In 1993 Dame Barbara had a standing invitation to visit Moscow but even with her iron constitution and indomitable will it was reckoned that such hazards as diphtheria and sniper fire around the parliament building made the trip too hazardous. Nevertheless the Russian publication of Barbara Cartland has begun. Likewise the Czech, the Bulgarian and the Hungarian. The Poles began in February 1992 with four titles a month each one selling twenty thousand copies.

And so it goes on. Contracts for Arabic editions were signed during the Gulf War. Japan sells twenty thousand copies of two titles every month. ('Other romantic lines fail in Japan as they have been considered too sexy for the readers', though my friend Professor Roy MacGregor Hastie, who is at the university in Osaka, is surprised by this because, he says, the specialist ladies' bookshops in Japan cater in special ladies' pornography. *Chacune à son goût*, I suppose.)

Icelandic, Faroese, Maltese, Hebrew, Romanian, Serbo-Croat . . . the languages appear unending. Ian has his work cut out wheeling and dealing, particularly because in so many of these emerging readerships the copyright laws count for less than nothing. In China, for example, where contracts were recently signed, he claims that some hundred and fifty Cartland titles have been 'pirated' and translated with no reference to his company – let alone payment. It makes it very difficult to negotiate a legitimate contract. Why should a fly Chinese publisher pay out good money when he can get away with publishing for free.

The same applies throughout the Far East, particularly in Indonesia, Korea and Thailand. In India the Dame was unamused on a recent visit at being mobbed by teenage fans all demanding her autograph on their pirate copies of her romances.

I have the evidence of this international phenomenon around me as I write. Cartland books and magazines in every conceivable language cover the top of my desk. Beautiful people in regency gear gaze adoringly into each other's eyes in editions from Paris to Frankfurt, Tokyo to Warsaw. It is strange how each nationality's jacket picture subtly distorts the original so that the Germans appear just a little more lantern jawed and teutonic, and the French more gamine and Gallic, than they would in the original English edition. Here, on the back jacket of a Japanese edition, the lovers look as if they have stepped from the *Mikado* or *Madama Butterfly*. Nothing too obvious, but his dapper dark looks, those high cheek bones and ever so slightly protruding teeth can surely not be English. And she, with that caked pale make-up and kohl black eyes, surely has more than a touch of the Geisha.

*Liebe auf Abwegen . . . 'Mein Name ist Castleton,' sagte Devina
. . . 'Ist das ein englischer Name? Ich kenne ihn nicht.'*

*Duello d'Amore . . . Vulcan House, in Grosvenor Square, e
Caroline vi risiedeva con una cigina che le faceva da chaperon,
l'Onorabile Mrs Edgmont.*

*La Valse des Coeurs . . . 'Richard! Est-ce à dire . . . que . . .
que nous allons nous marier maintenant?' . . . 'Des que nous serons
arrivés à Vienne,' repondit-il. 'J'aurai, alors le droit de vous protégér.'
. . . 'Oh, Richard!'*

This is the language of love in any language and Barbara
Cartland has used it to transmute her terribly English words
into international gold. At the end of 1992 Ian estimated that
his mother had sold six hundred million copies of her books
around the world. Even allowing for the prodigious number
of titles, this is quite a record.

Of the nearly six hundred books only five have been
filmed, the first by Ed Friendly in 1977 and the remaining
four by Gainsborough Films, financed and distributed by Sir
Lew Grade. Of the five only two have been shown in the UK,
confirmation that although she is one of the most famous
personalities in her native land her work is less appreciated
than almost anywhere. Has familiarity bred something in us?
Is she the victim of the prophet without honour in your own
country adage? Are we an unromantic lot? Obsessed with sex?

Certainly she seems to be a remarkable one-woman romantic export drive. But somehow home consumption is less
dramatic. A clear case of 'No Barbara Cartland please, we're
British'.

Chapter Thirteen

Barbara thinks men are wonderful. Here are three of the most wonderful men in her life. What were they really like? They are her brother Ronald, Lord Mountbatten and Peter Barber. Peter gave her lunch at Claridge's every Wednesday.

D ame Barbara is all about men.

Her attitude towards the opposite sex is perplexing, wilful and contrary, but it is perfectly plain that even in her nineties she luxuriates in male company and is never happier than when alone with a man. The men in her life have been vital; sometimes they have been almost as much fantasy as reality but they have shaped and formed her life and, at times, given it its purpose.

I wanted to pause and consider three of the more important.

Of all the men in Dame Barbara's life her brother Ronald is probably the most influential. They were very close and his death at Dunkirk in 1940 left a painful void.

I find it difficult to be certain about Ronald. He was plainly a man of promise and of courage and yet the Dame is such a plausible myth-maker that I approach him with a degree of caution. Could he really have been as gilded as she makes out? I felt I wanted some independent corroboration and yet his life was finished more than fifty years before I was conducting my researches. Besides which, it was essentially a life of promise rather than achievement. How could it be otherwise? He was only thirty-three years old when he died.

I wondered if Bill Deedes might be of assistance. Lord Deedes, better known as W.F. or Bill, had been editor at the *Daily Telegraph* when I used to write for them regularly. He had been a long-serving Tory MP after the war, but before the war he had been a lobby correspondent for the *Morning Post*. Looking at the dapper pin-striped figure of Ronald, staring out from the jacket of his sister's valedictory book, I was irresistibly reminded of Bill and felt instinctively that the two must have known each other and might possibly have been friends.

I was right. There were only six or so years' difference in age between them and Bill said that Ronald was his best friend in the House before the war when he was in the lobby. This is something he has rather carefully never admitted to Ronald's sister. Dame Barbara is not really Deedes's cup of tea, but then superficial evidence makes it quite surprising to discover that she was Ronald's cup of tea either.

'Ronald was the genuine article,' he said. 'In fact I still have a pair of shoes from Lobbs that I bought because they were like Ronald's.' The affection was obviously mutual because Bill recalls that when one of the other Birmingham seats – he thinks it may have been Austen Chamberlain's – became free Ronald tried to persuade Bill to put up for it.

'Ronald was easily the best dressed man in the lobby,' recalls Bill. 'Black jacket and always a fresh carnation every day.' And the shoes. 'He had a very long foot and the shoes were very black and shiny. I've never yet got mine to look quite like Ronald's.'

He remembers also 'the highly intelligent face' and 'the first rate mind' – surprising attributes, thinks Bill, in such a snappy dresser.

'He was a Rupert Brooke figure. He led from the front and he knew that some of us were going to be victims of appeasement. He wasn't fatalistic about it but it looked to him, as it looked to me, like a fair old cock-up. For me he stands out as the model – the symbol of a tragedy.'

I am in several minds about Lord Mountbatten and his part in Dame Barbara's life.

Here is the archetypal Cartland hero on the very last page of *Love at the Helm* as he contemplates the lovely Delora:

> Now he knew that she would be there always and for ever, and he would worship her because she had brought him the true, pure love for which all men seek as they voyage over the difficult, unpredictable and often tempestuous sea of life.
>
> 'I worship you,' he said against her lips.
>
> Then there was no further need for words.

This is very much par for the course. It is Cartland in C.S. Forester mode putting Hornblower through her romantic coffee-grinder. The hero, returning in 1815 from brilliant feats of derring-do, is even called Captain Horn. The jacket shows a dashing naval officer with sword, epaulettes and 'white kerseymere breeches' embracing a blonde in blue ('there was an unsophisticated and unspoilt innocence about her that he had never found in any woman and expected least of all to discover in the sister of the Fifth Earl of Scawthorn').

None of that is unexpected but there, sharing the billing with Dame Barbara's name above this nautical clinch, though in a typeface a notch or two smaller, is the name of one of the most famous sailors of the century, uncle of Prince Philip, 'Admiral of the Fleet, the Earl Mountbatten of Burma'.

Versatile though I knew him to be I had never realised that Mountbatten numbered the writing of historical romances among his talents. In fairness to him and Dame

Barbara, his name is prefaced with the words 'inspired and helped by'. Also, in the author's note the Dame explains that he 'helped me with the historical background of many of my novels'. And she adds that he wrote the preface to *Barbara Cartland's Book of Useless Information*.

I was sorry, on consulting Philip Ziegler's authorised and magisterial biography of Mountbatten, to find no mention of this literary activity. He does, however, make two references to Barbara, both intriguing.

The first is her description of being kissed by Mountbatten. Unlike the final scene in *Love at the Helm* there is no meeting of lips. He kissed her quite chastely on the cheek. Nevertheless, ' "A streak of fire ran through me as if I had been struck by lightning. It was a definitely painful yet ecstatic sensation. From a woman's point of view the power was devastating." From the moment Dickie fixed his eyes on her, spoke to her in that deep, amazingly attractive voice . . . she was his.'

Ziegler says, a little tongue-in-cheek, that 'Others less privileged than Mrs Cartland still found the impact of his personality almost overwhelming'.

What is remarkable, of course, is that Barbara's recorded impression of the kiss is so like the standard description of the kisses in her books. Did she really feel what she says she felt? Was she fantasising? Or romanticising? And what a shame that Ziegler never tells us what Mountbatten's thoughts were as he planted this astonishing peck on his old friend's cheek.

The other reference to Barbara in the Mountbatten biography is a wonderful case of mistaken identity. In old age he helped keep himself going by taking the pills. In his case, on Barbara's advice he took between three and five vitamin E capsules a day. Mentioning this to Sir Jules Thorn, the founder of the eponymous electrical giant, he commented on what a splendid person Barbara was.

Sir Jules was outraged. He said she was destroying the

National Health Service. Mountbatten said he found this hard to believe since she habitually wrote twenty novels a year and wouldn't have had time to destroy the Health Service even if she'd wanted to. Sir Jules then said that he was sure that Barbara had never written a novel in her life.

Only then did it transpire that he was talking about Barbara Castle.

Barbara Cartland talks with huge affection and admiration of Mountbatten and claims that in later life they were much in love, spoke every day on the telephone and that each morning to enable him to face the rigours of the day he used to play her the Royal Philharmonic Orchestra recording of 'Love Songs sung specially for you'. Barbara's rendition of 'Mr Wonderful' and 'Dream Lover' must have made all the difference. She was nearly eighty when she cut the disc but she carried it off. Indeed against all the odds there is a little-girl sibilance and charm to this preposterously geriatric enterprise. She sounds an amazingly young almost-eighty.

She and Lord Louis had known each other practically all their lives though it was Mountbatten's wife, the almost impossibly rich and glamorous Edwina, who had known Barbara first. Edwina was the daughter of a Conservative MP called Wilfred Ashley but her fortunes derived from her grandfather Sir Ernest Cassel. Cassel, son of a Cologne money-lender, had parlayed his way into an immense fortune and became Edward VII's financial eminence grise. After the death of his wife and daughter Edwina became, in Ziegler's words 'his principal interest'.

Barbara herself recalls the eight tons of Tuscany marble Cassel imported for Brooke House his 'massive mausoleum in Park Lane'. The marble hall was nicknamed 'The Giant's Lavatory'.

Edwina's energy emulated Barbara's for she was, in Philip Ziegler's words 'consumed by the daemons of duty and ambition'. It was she, of course, who recruited Barbara into the St John's Ambulance Brigade. Indeed it was while on a dauntingly onerous tour on behalf of St John's that she collapsed and died. In 1956 her doctor had told her that if she went on with her ridiculous work-load she would be dead within three years. She took a conscious decision to carry on as before and in February 1960 she died in Borneo. She was only fifty-nine years old.

Mountbatten's friends all expected him to remarry. He was not happy with his own company and even in late middle age he was inordinately attractive to women, though not much interested in sex. He adored their company but wasn't particularly keen on bed. (Unlike Edwina, alas!)

Ziegler says that there was 'no shortage of rich and well-connected women who would have been delighted to become the second Countess Mountbatten of Burma. Mountbatten may have played with the idea from time to time, but there is no reason to think that he ever considered it seriously.'

Maybe not, but there is no question that Mountbatten was an admirer of the Dame's. He was hard-up and lonely. She gave him lavish presents and she spoiled him. He came to Camfield for his birthday and she gave him hundreds of presents, small things, not lavish, but lots and lots all individually wrapped and tied with bows and set out on a sofa in the drawing-room. Mountbatten reacted like a little boy, unwrapping them all eagerly and exclaiming that he had never been given presents like this before. Nigel, the chef, baked a special cake decorated extravagantly with flags and ships.

In her published scrapbook – produced in aid of the Royal Photographic Society's Appeal, (she's always been generous with charity) – there are some snaps of Mountbatten being given his cake and another of him photographing the Dame who is saying cheese to camera while clutching her Pekinese rather roughly under her right arm. It all looks very cosy.

Who knows? Clearly they were friends. Clearly Dame Barbara invested him with many of the qualities she gave to her fictional romantic heroes. Clearly Mountbatten thought her admirable and was flattered by her attentions and her hospitality and generosity. But did he take her seriously? She says that she never seriously considered matrimony any more than he.

Ziegler himself told me that Dame Barbara took extreme umbrage about the Mountbatten book. She had received him with customary grace and enthusiasm when he went to Camfield Place to ask about Mountbatten but when the book appeared she responded with a half-page article in the *Daily Mail* which accused him of 'muck-raking'.

Ziegler took legal advice and was told that the piece was 'probably libellous'. However, he contented himself with a right of reply in which he said that Dame Barbara did not have a 'flicker of a sense of history'. Then, foolishly, he agreed to a television confrontation. His words, he says, are all right but his general deportment was agitated and nervous to a degree. His children videoed it and took huge delight in showing all and sundry 'Daddy on TV with Barbara Cartland'. In intellectual terms he wouldn't concede defeat but he has to admit that in visual terms he was made to look more than faintly ridiculous.

He suggests that this may have had something to do with Mountbatten's family's ambivalence about Dame Barbara. Mountbatten himself admired her as a personality and enjoyed her flattery and lavish presents. His daughters, he thinks, regarded her as a nuisance because she made Mountbatten look ridiculous by association. Dame Barbara thinks his family was 'jealous of the attention he paid her'. Her sheer force of personality is so extraordinary that whoever she touches becomes, *faute de mieux*, a character in her own fantastic invention. It is very difficult to think of a situation she would not dominate or at the very least of a show she would not steal.

Lady Pamela Hicks, the younger of Earl Mountbatten's two daughters, rather confirmed the Ziegler view.

'She was brought into the family by my aunt,' she said, 'and she became a friend. And after my mother died she and my father *were* friends and she did amuse him. She's such good company . . . but my sister and I have been rather disturbed since my father died to read that there might have been some sort of "romantic" interest. I'm afraid that's wishful thinking.'

Nevertheless after Ronald I think it is safe to say that Mountbatten came nearer to satisfying what one might call the Barbaronic ideal in her life.

She has always seemed to need men in her life and yet here, as everywhere, there are contradictions. On the one hand her men are ineffably tiresome because they won't do as she says and she knows best; yet on the other hand they are strong, virile, faultless, sweep you up into their arms and protect you from everything for ever and ever. You can't, I submit, have it both ways, though it doesn't, of course, prevent her from doing so.

Dame Barbara is, it goes almost without saying, one of the great survivors so that when I asked her who I should talk to about her and her life, she looked bleaker than usual. I would have loved to talk to a 'man in her life' but there was no one left. I had just been to the Requiem for Margaret, Duchess of Argyll. The Duchess had been memorialised in the press as if she were a relic of a forgotten age. The assembled journalists had watched the mourners at the Jesuit Church in Farm Street as if they were dinosaurs. As they shuffled in, dowagers and dukes, decrepit on their silver-topped canes, the young suits from Fleet Street looked on in ignorant amazement. This was history made, just, flesh.

Another world. For the modern generation of journalists that whole pre-war society scene was beyond imagination. Yet the Duchess was more than a decade younger than the Dame.

Margaret of Argyll, once a stunning society beauty, whose first wedding attracted a crowd of thousands, ended as a largely forgotten and abandoned figure. When she died most of the press coverage concentrated on a notorious divorce case featuring the Duchess wearing only a double string of pearls and fellating a naked, headless man. She belonged to Barbara's 'Dancing Years' and yet she was more than ten years Barbara's junior.

'Poor Margaret,' said Dame Barbara shaking her head. She had gone mad in the end, suffering under the illusion that she was not in a London nursing home but on board an ocean liner sailing round the world. Her trouble, according to Barbara, was that she never even opened a book in later years. Consequently her brain had addled. It was no good allowing the brain to rot. You had to stay active in every way. Nevertheless she wrote a kind article about Margaret in youth for the *Daily Mail* and didn't mention the headless man once. 'No one's interested in that, darling,' she said, wrongly, of course. But it was left to others to dish the dirt on the dead Duchess.

I should have got to the Duchess before she died but there were others to talk to. These were not contemporaries nor even people who went back a long way in her life; but there were one or two who had got to know her well in old age.

'You must talk to Peter,' she said.

'Peter?'

'Oh you know, darling. My boyfriend. We have lunch at Claridge's every Wednesday.'

I was startled. She had never mentioned him before. His

name was Peter Barber and he lived in Beaulieu. She said he had planted thousands of trees all over England and had just suffered some severe financial losses.

She gave me his address and a few days later he phoned in answer to my letter and suggested I visit him one day. Barbara was away in Scotland so the weekly lunch was in abeyance.

He met me at Southampton station, a stocky figure with white hair and a pinkish complexion which must have appealed to his friend. He was more than happy to talk quite frankly even on the drive to his home which turned out to be a large single-storey, architect-designed ranch-style house in the heart of the New Forest. It was on the market because of his sudden financial débâcle. He had lost a considerable amount of money because of a trust he had set up with a European bank. In effect the bank had stolen the money and he couldn't get it back. It sounded like a good story but it wasn't the one I had come to hear even though it made his weekly lunches at Claridge's look a bit problematic. He was the one who always paid.

I wasn't surprised. You wouldn't expect the Dame to go dutch.

There was one particular point that Barber wanted to make absolutely clear. He was not Dame Barbara's 'boy-friend'.

'She treats me as if I was,' he said, 'and she talks about me as if I was. But look, I may be seventy-eight years old but if I did have a girlfriend she'd be nineteen not ninety.'

'Tell her', said Mrs Barber, a little later, 'that he has a wife.'

Mrs Barber has never actually met Dame Barbara.

He was one of those men transformed by the war. A Staffordshire lad, he was commissioned from the ranks into the Royal Artillery, then transferred to the gunners where he was a brother officer and friend of Edmund Rothschild of the great banking family. After the war Eddy Rothschild said to Barber that he now had to learn about banking and he thought it would be a good idea if Peter learned about estate management. He wanted him to be the Rothschild agent and so for thirty years Peter Barber acted as Rothschild's manager in everything outside the bank. With his cousin Brigadier John Lucas-Phillips he has written a tree book, a shrub book and a successful work on 'Rothschild Rhododendrons'.

In the course of this career he met a large number of rather grand people including a neighbour, 'Lord Louis', Earl Mountbatten of Burma, an old flame (or not) of Dame Barbara. He and Mountbatten became friendly. Mountbatten used to seek out the Barbers for a bit of company. He would simply ring when he was at a loose end and come round, usually at the weekend. Sometimes the two men would go up to London on a jaunt. 'Dickie was a funny man,' says Barber. 'He'd had that wonderful career. And you *knew* he was a great man, yet when you got to know him he seemed really quite ordinary.'

After Mountbatten was blown up in his boat by the IRA in 1979 Barber walked into Claridge's one day to find Barbara sitting in the lounge. He had never met her but – unsurprisingly – recognised her at once and, knowing that she had been a close friend of Mountbatten's, he approached her to commiserate. 'I said "We've both just lost a great friend" and she put her arms round me, more or less.'

Then later, Mountbatten's former secretary, John Barratt, wrote a book about his old master. Dame Barbara helped him with it and in this connection wrote to Barber. The Wednesday lunches stemmed from this and soon turned into a regular fixture.

She always had the same: smoked salmon with a thick creamy sauce with the salmon sliced so thin, Barber says, it's hardly there. Then a Dover sole, grilled, with another creamy sauce. Never a pudding but a plate of petits fours. She used to have white wine or champagne but for the last two or three years she has eschewed alcohol and has a small bottle of still mineral water followed by many cups of coffee. Barber for his part tends to have beef from the trolley and he drinks wine.

She ticks him off for drinking too much and gives him advice about his financial problems. He says that he hardly says a word. She loves to talk about the Royal Family and is usually excellently informed. Most of her royal stories come true in the papers two or three weeks after. Otherwise she will talk about events of the day, her latest campaign, Raine. And so on. I recognised the list.

They always have the best table, number one, just inside the door. The next one, until his death about a year earlier, was nearly always occupied by Charles Sweeney, Margaret Argyll's first husband, beside whom she now lies (contrary to her wishes) in Brookwood Cemetery.

'The staff worship her,' says Barber. She is very good at remembering special occasions and giving them little presents, usually an autographed book. He makes no secret of the fact that he enjoys watching this grand old hotel 'turn itself upside down for her'. The lunches always last much the same time – about an hour and a half.

It's rather a charming ritual though it seemed, from Peter Barber's end, to be going through a period of slight strain when I met him. There's no question his wife was none too keen on it, especially since the disaster with the family fortune. There seemed every prospect that they would move off to Italy and live on the Calabrian estate of a son-in-law, in which case the Wednesday lunches would presumably go. But even a day out from Hampshire and lunch at Claridge's burns a hole in the pocket when you've suddenly lost three and a half million. In the event, sadly, he did move to Italy and communication between the two became largely telephonic.

Barber enjoys the company of the rich and famous and sometimes the slightly scandalous. Rothschilds apart, one of his greatest friends was Charlie Clore. He knew Vivien Leigh in Cairo; he knew Stephen Ward. He knew the Archbishop of Canterbury. His range was wide.

Barbara for her part was lonely and she liked the romantic idea of a man some fifteen years her junior giving her a weekly lunch in a hotel which, with its somewhat faded old dowager charms, is familiar and cherished and, in a sense, an old, old friend. She enhanced the relationship with a little of her romantic imagination, teased it perhaps into something a little more meaningful than it really was. She's good at that.

In a way and to an extent she has always done that sort of thing with her men.

No real man could ever live up to her romantic imagination, and yet, in that imagination, that is precisely what they do.

Chapter Fourteen

I read some of her novels. What are they really like? Another romantic novelist says that sometimes they can be a 'little tacky'. An American academic thinks Barbara is 'a trailblazer'. She has written all sorts of other books as well. She is a 'generic'.

T he Barbara Cartland novels
are nowadays seldom, if ever, reviewed in serious newspapers
nor, as far as I know, anywhere else. Her two earlier
biographers have attempted some literary analysis, though it
is scarcely critical; and Dr Joseph McAleer, in his historical
monograph on 'Popular Reading and Publishing in Britain
1914–1950' makes a number of telling points.

But generally speaking, Cartland books escape the critical
net and although the chattering classes have a uniform and
highly patronising view of the books they are seldom if ever
based on an actual first-hand reading. It must be said, incidentally, that there is something of a dichotomy within the
Dame herself. When addressing her reading public she never
suggests that her books are anything other than worth while.
It would, of course, be commercial folly to do anything else.
In private, at least with me, she takes an altogether more
robust view. After all, it was she herself who told me not
to bother with them on the grounds that they were all the
same.

My impression is that while she would defend her work on
grounds of style, accuracy of research and detail, and general

all-round professionalism she acknowledges, within her own circle, that they are merely artefacts designed to give whole-some, harmless pleasure to what in a former age would have been servants and shop girls. She herself is perfectly happy writing her romances but she's not the sort of person you'd expect to find reading one.

I suppose that before embarking on this study I was as ignorant yet opinionated as anyone else. In other words I had never read a Barbara Cartland novel but I 'knew' that they were sloppy and sentimental, set in a sort of pseudo-historical world in which the girls wore ball gowns and the men frock-coats; that there was always an unspeakable cad who came to a sticky end; that the heroine was a virgin; and that she gets the hero in the end. I had a suspicion that early in the plot the hero might have been subverted by some sort of seductive witch though I was not too sure about this. I 'knew' that there was no overt sex.

That was about it.

I decided that before trying to assess the *oeuvre* and to consider what people like Henry Cloud and Gwen Robyns had said, to balance perception against actuality, to seek the views of publishers and competing authors, I really ought to read at least one book – whatever she herself might advise.

I thought it best to start with a more or less contemporary work so I chose a later Cartland, *Love and War*. I liked the Tolstoyan echoes of the title while wondering if they were deliberate. The cover picture on my American edition showed a blonde in a ball gown gently embracing a dark-haired man in a dark-blue Bullingdon frock-coat. She has her eyes shut and he is kissing her gently on the cheek. Very gently. They are framed in a golden draped curtain and beyond the window is a lot of golden sunlight and a sort of herbaceous border full of daisies. Above the heavy black BARBARA CARTLAND it says 'A New Camfield Novel of Love. 105'.

Inside there is a message from the Dame saying, inter alia, that 'It is easy here to write of love and I know you will enjoy the Camfield Novels of Love. Their plots are definitely exciting and the covers very romantic. They come to you, like all my books, with love.'

She signs off with a 'Bless You'.

Next comes an 'Author's Note' which, more or less, is designed to let the reader know that the historical background is accurate. The story is set in the spring of 1813. The scene is England but in the background is the Peninsular War and the first British victories against the French. Dame Barbara drops the name of Sir Arthur Bryant – very much her sort of historian – and his book *The Age of Elegance*. Sir Arthur specialised in popular narrative, was much derided by serious academic historians and yet was – in a prosaic way – perfectly sound.

Dame Barbara is clearly proud of her historical accuracy but the historical information in this book is not hugely complicated. Thus, 'The predilection of the Prince Regent for the Arts was well-known in Bath' or, of Napoleon, 'He had risen from Corporal to Emperor and his ambition was to conquer the world.' You don't need a history degree to be able to produce sentences such as these. On the other hand they are, up to their point, perfectly accurate.

The plot goes more or less like this:

Young Gina Langdale has just returned from Finishing School (Dame Barbara is lavish if eccentric with her capital letters) to live with her widowed mother, Lady Langdale. Her Ladyship is a simple, mildly dotty soul, who was protected from life by her immensely wise husband.

Gina misses her father. (In Cartlandese 'father', naturally, has a capital 'F'.)

Lady L. has become infatuated with young Captain Guy Dawes of the Household Cavalry. He looks suspiciously like a Cad. Gina suspects him of stealing the family snuff boxes.

Despairingly Gina turns to the dashing Marquis of Mortlake who was invalided out of the Household Cavalry – the Life Guards actually. Coincidentally young Dawes and Gina's father are also of the same regiment. Mortlake was shot in the shoulder by the French.

He is having an affaire with Imogen Strangway, the infamous femme fatale.

The Marquis promises to help Gina and invites her, her mother and Dawes to a party at Arrowhead his very old, very beautiful family home.

At the party Gina demonstrates that she is not only jolly pretty, but also jolly bright – she talks knowledgeably to Lord Castlereagh of all people, at dinner. She also shows that she is a superb horsewoman.

Lady Imogen starts to become jolly jealous of Gina.

The Marquis discovers Major Dawes cheating at cards. He orders him to go to the fighting in the Peninsula. If he doesn't he'll be drummed out of the Regiment in disgrace.

That evening, while everybody is dancing, smugglers arrive at the bottom of the garden. Gina sees Lady Imogen talking to the chief smuggler. They are French and Lady Imogen is a Spy.

Lady Imogen hands the head smuggler a note. In return the smuggler gives Lady Imogen a flask of special potion which will render the person who drinks it her slave for twenty-four hours.

Gina warns the Marquis.

When Lady Imogen slips some of the magic potion into his champagne he switches round the glasses.

Lady Imogen swallows her drink and drops down dead.

Gina's mother becomes engaged to a nice older man.

Gina and the Marquis embrace and tell each other that they love each other and they agree to be married.

The last paragraph in the book says, 'She must start making herself look beautiful because the most wonderful man in the world was coming to dinner.'

And that's it.

Plot summaries tend to be unfair and it would be perfectly possible to make *War and Peace* look as banal as *Love and War* but I think mine is a reasonable description of the book's salient points. The crucial facts are that the hero is very handsome and very experienced. We are told that 'Because he was so handsome, the Marquis had been pursued from the moment he left Eton. Before he had been sent abroad he had indulged in a number of *Affaires de Coeur*.'

'Affaires de Coeur' indeed! What the Dame is really saying is that Marquis has slept around and is very good in bed.

The heroine, on the other hand, is deeply wonderful in every way but also a virgin. The Marquis knows this and says 'He wanted to teach her about love, of which he was aware she knew nothing'.

I don't think the Dame quite means 'love' here. It's plain that young Gina knew about real love because she loved her father to distraction and loved her mother quite a lot as well. My view is that the Dame doesn't mean 'love' she means 'sex'. She can't say so out loud in the sort of books she writes but what the reader is intended to understand is that the Marquis is going to teach Gina how to have multiple orgasms.

There is a problem here. At least I detect a problem if the Dame is setting herself up as a guardian of Moral Rectitude and I think she does. As Joseph McAleer said to me, 'From her first novel [*Jigsaw*, 1923] Cartland has been a moraliser, devoting long sections of narrative to the wicked consequences for a girl if she forsakes her innocence in a cruel world. Her personal crusade against pre-marital sex has inspired some graphic prose; she has compared the loss of virginity, for example, to a crucifixion . . . she used, and continues to use, her novels as her own personal pulpit.'

In the course of writing this book I mentioned the Dame to my friend Margaret Pemberton, author of a number of romantic sagas and a former President of the Romantic Novelists' Association. Margaret is sensible and balanced and I was therefore quite surprised at the heat of her criticism of the Dame's writing. When she had finished I asked if she would mind putting her case in writing.

She did, and this is what she wrote:

In a Cartland novel the heroines are young and virginal, the heroes are older and sexually experienced (there is no hint, in any Cartland novel, that when the hero finally sweeps the heroine off to the bridal chamber he will fumble, or be inept). Never, however, does Miss Cartland state where this sexual expertise (which she obviously finds attractive and realises her readers will also find attractive) has been gained.

In the social world Miss Cartland depicts the answer is a little tacky (which is no doubt why Miss Cartland skates so smoothly over the subject, tackiness not being part and parcel of a Cartland novel). With no single young ladies of their own class willing to risk their reputations by being sexually co-operative, many young gentlemen of the day happily foraged among working-class young women who could be overawed or intimidated into complaisance (especially when the young women in question were employees in the family home and non-cooperation on their part carried with it the threat of dismissal). Another well-honed path to sexual prowess lay in professional tuition (the number of prostitutes in the era of which Miss Cartland writes beggared belief). But by no means least, as it was generally accepted that once an upper-class young lady married she was free to dispense with her sexual favours in whatever direction might take her fancy (though discreetly of course), the way was open for the young bucks of the day to sow their wild oats to their hearts' content.

Such arrangements were tickety-boo for the upper classes (whose daughters remained assiduously protected), but were rather less attractive for those without upper-class clout.

In a novel purporting to do nothing more than entertain, none of this would matter (and Miss Cartland does entertain and on a mass scale). What jars, however, is her much-stated conviction that the morality of her novels is a morality that should still be aspired to, especially when that morality has only ever been depicted by her from one very prejudiced viewpoint (prostitution and adultery having as little place in a Cartland novel as Einstein's Theory of Relativity). And when reading the last chapter of a Cartland novel, where the hero sweeps the heroine off her feet and into the bridal-chamber, doesn't it rather take the gilt off the gingerbread to realise that, if historical accuracy were to rear its ugly head, chances are the hero is just about to give the heroine a dose of the clap?

Something of the sort had occurred to me too and it certainly seemed a point worth putting to Dame Barbara.

I did so in writing, rather hoping that I might get a considered, written response. Alas, she did not reply until our next meeting, when sitting alongside me on the sofa she launched into an irritated attack on Margaret and her ignorance of history. Unfortunately it became clear after a few moments that Dame Barbara was not talking about gonorrhea, syphilis, genital herpes or any other sexually transmitted disease or infections of the eighteenth and nineteenth centuries but about AIDS. AIDS, she told me splenetically, had only been discovered in about 1970 and therefore it was absolute poppycock to suggest that any of her gallant heroes could possibly have been stricken with it. My correspondent simply didn't know what she was talking about. In any case if someone did discover that he was suffering from venereal disease he did the honourable thing and went out and shot himself. Chaps were always going out and shooting themselves in the good old days when men were men and had a sense of what being a man was all about.

And before I knew where I was and before I could even

mouth a feeble, 'No but . . .' or 'Surely gonorrhea . . .' we were off on one of the Dame's characteristic and unstoppable streams of consciousness and I was, once again, defeated but mesmerised, just as I felt Dr Anthony Clare had been when he had her in his psychiatrist's chair.

But one mustn't take the Cartland books *too* seriously.

On the credit side I thought *Love and War* raced along at a very snappy pace and it had great charm in a mildly loopy way. There is something after all to be said for having villains who are really villainous and heroes and heroines who are seriously heroic. Dame Barbara deploys a sort of short-hand formula for describing people which leaves the reader's imagination full rein. Thus, 'He was a distinguished looking man'. This says virtually nothing about the chap except that he is a goody. The reader is free to invent and imagine the way in which he looks distinguished with none of the constraints of more serious writers who will spend an age describing physiognomy in what can, let's face it, be very boring detail. 'Distinguished' is a very Cartland word, as is 'pretty' for women. This also is a word which leaves practically everything to the imagination. Thus 'Gina saw that all the Ladies were extremely pretty and the Gentlemen distinguished'. (This is a genuine quotation, not a fabrication.)

Words like 'pretty', 'lovely' and 'enjoying' have a simple imprecision which is easy to read. Odd, therefore, suddenly to stumble across longer ones such as 'iridescent', 'egotistical' and 'redolent'. They seem out of place. They occur infrequently and yet sufficiently regularly to make one think that they are there for a purpose. I guess that another effect of them is to make the reader feel that what she – most of them must surely be shes – is reading is more demanding than it actually is.

In terms of style and construction I was vividly reminded

of working on the *Daily Express* in the sixties when the hand of Dame Barbara's mentor, the late Lord Beaverbrook, still lay heavy on the paper he had created. Beaverbrook believed in short words, short sentences and short paragraphs.

The first chapter of *Love and War* runs to twenty-six pages. The print is well leaded so there are comparatively few words on the page yet in that first chapter there are no fewer than three hundred and thirty-five separate paragraphs. The shortest is three words – 'He kissed her' – and the longest I can find is fifty-one words. That paragraph contains four whole sentences which is very nearly a record. The effect is staccato and it is easy to believe that the whole has been dictated from the *chaise-longue* at the rate of several thousand words a day.

I think it reasonably safe to say that *Love and War* is fairly typical of later Cartland which is to say Cartland since the seventies. This means easily the greater number of novels since, as she is proud of boasting, she had 'written' a mere hundred by the time she was seventy. It was only then that she really slipped into gear and started to churn them out at the prodigious rate she has maintained into her nineties and which has earned her her place in the *Guinness Book of Records*.

The popular conception is that *all* her books are historical romances yet this is far from the truth. Earlier novels were different. *Jigsaw*, the very first, was set in Mayfair, the world she knew best. The heroine, described by Henry Cloud as 'a self-portrait, romantically enhanced, of Barbara herself' is a sort of innocent at large in a world full of the 'heinous perversions of man' (she used longer and more difficult words in those days).

Virginal Mona meets a man at a party. The man, unidentified, has 'dark hair . . . broad brow . . . two dark eyes' (these manage to glint, mock and laugh intermittently which is no mean feat). The mouth and jaw are both 'firm' though the rest of the face is irresponsible and he smiles back at her 'scrutiny' in a manner which is 'attractively impertinent'.

The man drives her away to a hill behind Wimbledon where he kisses her briefly on the lips with his firm mouth and takes her back to the party. Then Mona meets another man. This one *is* identified and turns out to be the Marquis of Leadenhall, heir to the Duke of Glenac. He falls in love with Mona but Mona does not fall in love with him. Too dull. Nevertheless she fancies being a Duchess and plights her troth, swiftly being rewarded by the death of the old Duke. The next thing she knows Mona is introduced to her brother-in-law, Alec, and realises that he is the man with the firm mouth who kissed her outside Wimbledon.

Mona fancies Alec and is frankly bored with her husband, the Duke. 'If only he would lose his temper, be brutal or abusive, Mona felt she would adore him. The eternal considerateness and kindness towards her simply rasped on her nerves.'

These are dodgy sentiments and it is no surprise that they themselves rasped on the nerves of generations of women, and not simply the later feminists whom Dame Barbara came to deride. Mona is saying that she longs for her husband to be 'brutal or abusive'. She hates him being considerate and kind. In other words part of her at least wants to be treated rough by an out-and-out shit.

In the end Mona does her duty but with a heavy heart. She loves the old bore with 'the affection of a child for a guardian' but without 'passion' or 'heart-breaking thrill'. She'd much prefer to take her chances with the brutal brother but she knows, alas, that a girl has to do what a girl has to do.

Later novels also took place in contemporary settings and some took themselves surprisingly seriously. None did so more than *Sleeping Swords* published in 1942 under her married name. The *Daily Telegraph* described it as 'long, serious' and 'well done'; the *Manchester Guardian* opined that she had adopted a 'Wells formula' and given us a 'socio-political novel, this time concerned with the last four decades of English history'.

I don't think that anyone, then or now, would claim that *Sleeping Swords* was a great novel but it had aspirations to genuine seriousness and some people liked it. The *Daily Sketch*, for instance, described it as a 'thoroughly enjoyable life-like romance of serious and controversial interest'. The paper added as a sort of postscript, 'Author known also as Barbara Cartland'.

Although this was her most pretentious novel it was not the only one over which she took time and for which she had hopes. She once said of herself (1964) that 'the moment I start writing with a pen I'm afraid I get rather pompous'. This may be true and certainly her dictated novels are very far from pomposity. But whether or not 'pompous' is the right word, it seems to me that the young and youngish Barbara took herself quite seriously as a writer in a way which the nonagenarian Dame simply does not.

Not that this view was always shared by critics. I particularly enjoyed the *Telegraph* man writing that *Desperate Defiance*, her 1936 novel, was 'A safe distance from everyday life' with its 'disreputable monks who wear red and yellow tam-o'-shanters'. The reviewer's final, brutal put-down, was that 'Even for a book of this kind the mortality among the characters seemed to be unusually high'.

On the other hand the same paper thought the central character of her 1939 book, *Self Made Hero* was a 'fine portrait'. Like *Sleeping Swords* it clearly has a serious dimension, at least as far as the central character is concerned. He is Morgan Wright, owner of Wright's World Wide Cheap Tailors, who is rejected by society until someone called Kit Combe decides to marry him.

'Here', said the *Telegraph*, 'is a character demanding pity and admiration: the sensitive, introspective, idealistic man, miserably lonely, hating pretentiousness, carrying the weight of his riches with dignity and courage.'

This sounds almost like an early Jeffrey Archer.

In his book Joseph McAleer describes Dame Barbara as 'certainly the most famous and successful author of romantic fiction in Britain and, indeed, the world'.

She has achieved this, argues McAleer, because she has 'refused to follow the changing tastes of readers and modernise her "Victorian" values'. By doing so she has made herself the Mrs Whitehouse of fiction. Publishers, she told McAleer, 'kept on saying, "Oh, come on Barbara, you must *really* be up to date", and I said, "*No*". That's why I write in the past. Everyone's a virgin in the past; it was all right.'

'Herein', continues McAleer, 'lay the compromise: in order to continue writing about virginal single women in a changing world, especially after the Second World War, Cartland had to abandon contemporary romance for historical romance. Since 1948, every one of her novels has been set in the period 1790–1914. Ironically, the past, which used to be the source for bawdier plotlines (*Forever Amber* is one example), has been used by Cartland as a kind of distant Eden.'

McAleer was the administrator at Hawthornden Castle, the Scottish writers' retreat owned by Drue Heinz, the well-known literary patronne. I had spent a month there and knew him well enough to tease out some supplementary thoughts.

'Personality and style' were the distinguishing Cartland characteristics he identified – in that order. She was, in his words, 'the most famous woman in the popular publishing industry, a self-made publicity machine who has amassed a considerable fortune and an international reputation as the "Queen of Romance". Because of her entrepreneurial spirit she has been jeered at by many.'

McAleer is surely right in suggesting that the Dame's personality and literary style are so intertwined. She writes as she is; she is as she writes.

'I consider her a trailblazer,' says McAleer. 'Today, popular novelists like Jeffrey Archer and Barbara Taylor Bradford are conspicuous by their media appearances to hype their latest book. Cartland was there first.'

Frances Whitehead, former Editorial Director of Mills and Boon, the publishers, who have produced books by practically every other romantic novelist in the world except for Dame Barbara, almost stands this idea on its head. In the old days there were several romantic novelists – Denise Robins, Ursula Bloom, Berta Ruck – who had the sort of flamboyant, fur-coat and Rolls-Royce star quality of Barbara Cartland. In the old days, says Ms Whitehead, that sort of writer would lord it over their publishers, insisting on lunch at the Ritz and no editorial interference with their wonderful words. 'They were Queens of Romance,' says Whitehead. 'But now the grey accountants have taken over.' Nowadays there is only one romantic novelist with that sort of outsize star quality: Dame Barbara. As Frances Whitehead puts it, 'She never dwindled into a mere author.'

'What sells is publicity,' she told McAleer. 'You can't buy what you haven't heard of.'

In her little pink promotional pamphlet she lists every one of her titles. The vast bulk are, of course, novels but it is instructive to see how much else she has written. They are listed after the fiction, under the heading, 'Her Other Wonderful Books'. (The more I study the Dame the more I remember her son's remark that no one sends her up as well as herself!)

The other 'wonderful books' include one volume of 'philosophy' (*Touch the Stars*) and two of biography. There are twelve history books along such predictable lines as *The Private*

Life of Charles II, *The Outrageous Queen* (the story of Christina of Sweden) and *Metternich – the Passionate Diplomat*. She has written twenty works of what she calls, a touch portentously 'Sociology'. These include two books on Etiquette, a *Book of Charm*, *Look Lovely*, *Be Lovely* and *Men are Wonderful*. None of these seem likely to be 'sociology' in quite the conventional meaning of the word.

She has compiled five cookbooks including *Recipes for Lovers* in which her trusty chef, Nigel Gordon, contributes the recipes and Dame Barbara comments as well as providing typical lovers' situations in which a meal seems called for. Thus, 'Stella is fair, slight, sensitive and a little shy. Michael is attracted to her but afraid of frightening her if he is too impetuous.'

Michael gives her watercress soup, chicken with pineapple and a strawberry mousse. With it they drink 'Pouilly Blanc Fumé'. Barbara comments on the mentally enlivening quality of cress and the healthy qualities of strawberries and says, 'If Michael treats Stella with tenderness and appeals to her imagination, he will win her heart and soul.'

All these romantic, or potentially romantic, situations are what one might loosely describe as 'moral' except for this:

'Desmond has for some months been in love with Isobel, who is older than himself and is married to a business tycoon who is always abroad.

'Daringly he asks her to dinner at a small French restaurant near his lodgings.'

'Daringly'? What *can* she mean? They dine off braised turbot in champagne, veal à la crème and Loukmades or Love Cakes with Honey. The Dame then tells us that Turbot is Imperial, that 'veal assists sexual activity' and Loukmades has 'been eaten by Greek lovers for centuries'.

Then, she says, 'Desmond's love-making must be as imaginative and original as the dinner he has chosen.'

In the context of Dame Barbara's moral crusading this is surely not quite right. Here is Desmond taking a married woman out to dinner while her husband is abroad on business and here is the Dame urging him to be 'imaginative' and 'original' in his love-making to her. Whatever happened to morality?

Once more it is simply no use expecting Barbara Cartland to be consistent in the conventional sense. Better really just to turn the pages and contemplate a dinner of 'Trout in Pink Coat, Pink Chicken and Strawberry Ice Cream with Hot Raspberry Sauce' accompanied by 'Lanson Pink Champagne or Vin Rosé'.

Her comment? 'A Pink dinner is a lovely way of celebrating the first time you met or the first time you made love. Have pink candles on the table and pink flowers, pink table-napkins, and of course wear a pink dress.'

After which there is really nothing to say. In matters gastronomic as in matters literary she is really beyond criticism.

After the cookbooks she lists two 'dramas', a radio operetta called *The Rose and the Violet*, a radio play about Elizabeth, Empress of Austria, five volumes of autobiography, a magazine, a 'special publication' (this is *Love at the Helm* aided and abetted by Lord Mountbatten, of which more elsewhere), five films, a book of verse (*Lines on Life and Love*) in which she tells her readers that 'Poetry is the music of prose and often it is the only method by which we can express our emotions'. Finally, under 'General', she includes a rag-bag of scrapbooks, cartoons, prayers, and *Useless Information* (Mountbatten again). Then come the four videos and that's it.

Never mind the quality, consider the quantity. I estimate just over sixty books other than the novels.

'Nobody writes purer or duller romantic fiction than she does these days,' says Dr McAleer and you could apply a similarly harsh verdict to many of the rest of her books. On the other hand they nearly all have a certain Cartland quality, a vivacity, a verve, an excess which reflects their creator's rosy, glowing, pink over-the-top-ishness quite accurately.

She gets quite cross when linked with Mills and Boon just as Mills and Boon become irritable when linked with her. In fact Mills and Boon *have* published the Dame but only in Spain and Holland where they were asked specifically for something set in the Regency period and Cartland was all they could think of.

'The point', says Frances Whitehead, 'is that we're both "generics". Mills and Boon have the *Good Housekeeping* seal of approval for Romantic Fiction. But if you want a Historical Romance set in the Regency Period it *has* to be Barbara Cartland.

'She's unique.'

Chapter Fifteen

Barbara asks me to join her at the Indian High Commission. She is helping to launch some cosmetics. Her interest in healing and health, and honey and vitamins began in the 1930s. However she likes to eat well.

I grew to love the Dame's letters.

They combined effusion with briskness. The phone and fax numbers in dark pink at an angle on the upper left-hand side, crest and address top centre, and above them at the very top, typed in, the legend, 'From: Dame Barbara Cartland, DBE, D. St J.' and below the text, in what appeared to be a blood-red felt tip, 'Love, Barbara Cartland'. A very firm and forward-sloping hand, particularly for one so old.

In May 1993 she wrote,

My Dear Mr Heald,

I wonder whether it would amuse you to come to see the wonderful new Cosmetics which have come through from India.

In the old days I always gave them to Indira Gandhi, and now Princess Shahnaz Husain is bringing them to England.

We have just had a huge success in Paris where a thousand people turned up. She is now having a Special Party at the Indian High Commission, India House, Aldwych, London WC2, on Wednesday next, 12 May, at 12 noon.

It would be wonderful if you could join us.

Please do come if you can.

Given the circumstances, indeed even without being given the circumstances, this was an irresistible invitation.

And so to the Indian High Commission arriving a little late to find the High Commissioner, dapper and pukka in that Doon School Anglophile fashion which puts most Englishmen to shame, in full flow. To be honest I took in less of the content than the style. It seemed to me the standard suave paean that any half decent diplomat would produce on such an occasion. I did catch something about 'humane, aesthetic approach' which was par for the course. It tied in with the Dame's longstanding predilection for all things natural.

Behind the podium were large photographs of Nehru and Gandhi. On the dais sat a fleshy Indian woman in a sari whom I took to be Princess Shahnaz Husain herself, a beaming Ian McCorquodale looking every inch the businessman in his pin-stripe suit, and of course Dame Barbara herself. By now I had almost ceased to marvel at her appearance but she was looking more than usually magnificent, her pink outfit and cream make-up, topped off with what looked like an enormous cerise lampshade. The auditorium was crammed with friends, hacks, cameramen and a TV crew from an American showbiz channel.

The Dame didn't make a formal speech but Ian spoke on her behalf explaining to the audience, a touch ingenuously, that 'I'm Ian McCorquodale and this is my mother here in pink'. Dame Barbara smiled and fluttered her caterpillar eyelashes.

Later there were photographs and interviews before everyone went through to another room where they were serving drinks and canapés. Leafing through the 'Legendary Shahnaz Herbal Range', I discovered to my pleasure that in between 'Forever Beautiful' (Age to Youth Day and Night Creams) and 'Sharose' (Rose Skin Tonic) was 'Barbara Cartland'

(Honey-Rose-Mint Moisture Plus). This was described as 'A powerful moisturiser, enriched with rose, mint, sandalwood, basil and honey. Porcelains the skin and restores its youthful qualities. A luxurious moisturising treatment'. 'Porcelains the skin,' I mused, contemplating the Dame's own remarkable complexion.

'Shahnaz has a passion for beauty,' Dame Barbara once wrote, 'and being beautiful herself, wants every other woman to look beautiful too.' This seemed dubious.

But just as I was considering it, I found myself talking to Ian and heard him ask, 'Does Mother know you're here?'

'No,' I said, flinching rather. On the whole I did not share Dame Barbara's exuberant penchant for publicity and I had an uneasy feeling that if I was not careful I would find myself in on her act whether I liked it or not.

I was right.

'Mother,' called Ian, 'Tim's here.'

She seemed delighted. Kiss on both cheeks. General roseate effusion. And then to my horror she took me firmly by the arm and turned to the press corps with a command to gather round and take a photograph of her with the young (!) man who is going to write '*my*' book.

My hair was too long and flopping over my eyes and I had dandruff on my collar, so as we posed Dame Barbara was plucking bits and pieces off my jacket and muttering 'Push your hair back, dear!' Photographs were taken, film was shot, and subsequently the man from American showbiz TV conducted a brief interview. Hostages, I thought, to fortune. Or as a mischievous friend remarked, 'Now you'll be in *Private Eye* for ever.'

The reason for her association with these curious Indian cosmetics was that, in the words of her biographer John Pearson/aka Henry Cloud, 'Soon after her fiftieth birthday she discovered one of the most important roles of her life –

and what was virtually a new unpaid career – as the country's Queen of Health, and patron saint of vitamins.' (Despite the essentially hagiographic nature of his work Pearson's waspish irreverence does sometimes shine through.)

In fact the Cartland health kick started well before then. She was in her late twenties when she first 'studied Herbal Medicine with the famous Mrs Leyel of Culpeper'. One of her little pink books, *Barbara Cartland's Health Experience*, sets out the chronology.

The early thirties were a bad time for her. All her life she had been brought up to believe that one married and lived happily ever after. Yet after the dazzling dancing years of her twenties she suddenly found herself as the no-longer-quite-so-young mother of a little girl rather than the boy she would have much preferred. Youth was over and she was no longer 'Flaming Youth' or 'Bright Young Person'. Like Ronald she was intrigued by clairvoyance, the occult, 'An Experiment with Time', and what, according to her the Chinese call 'The World Behind the World'.

Despite their apparently conventional upper-middle-class background and behaviour they were both in some respects quite cranky. Or at least to the bourgeoisie they seemed cranky and it was therefore no surprise when a depressed Barbara, laid low by colitis, fetched up in a Temple of Healing near Olympia. A friend of hers had been there and was under the impression that she had had an inflamed appendix removed by spirit surgery.

In an upper room bathed in blue light, Barbara was attended by a white-dressed woman in a deep trance who diagnosed 'an inflammation in your body' and prescribed a spoonful of olive oil three or four times a day. After a while the entranced woman in white announced that 'Healing rays have been poured into you and restoration has begun'.

Up to a point. The colitis improved but only a little and so Barbara approached Mrs Leyel at Culpeper's. It was Mrs Leyel who first told her about ginseng. Also that sorrel will 'cure the blood', that butcher's broom will sort out headaches, parsley and pimpernel will deal with kidney ailments and borage 'inflammations'. If this last was true it is surprising that the Olympia medium only prescribed olive oil. In any event it is from this period that her commitment to 'alternative medicine' began.

Mrs Leyel was, according to her, 'an entrancing person. One had only to speak to her to be enthused by her love of healing, by the aura of kindness she emitted to all who consulted her, by the fund of knowledge that seemed to bubble out of her with every subject she spoke on.'

As so often, however, the Cartland behaviour and beliefs were unpredictable. At about the same time as she was converted to ginseng and Culpeperism there was a craze for slimming. In her no-nonsense fashion she declared that 'a silly fad began to affect the national health'. She herself was plump, which men seemed to like. Besides she said, 'Quite frankly, I like eating, I enjoy a good meal, and I can't work if I don't eat.' When slimming was at its most fashionable she had a lunch in Upper Brook Street consisting of chopped raw cabbage and carrot, an egg yolk and a strip of lean bacon, served by a butler and two footmen. She protested and was reluctantly given bread and cheese. On another occasion she lunched with Anna May Wong at her flat in Sloane Square. The meal consisted of 'scraps of fish cooked in a peculiar way' followed by very small mandarin oranges eaten with a stick. As soon as the meal was over she walked across the square and had 'a good juicy chop' at Peter Jones.

'I'm afraid', she said, 'I shall never be thin and quite frankly I don't care a damn.'

Is there a discrepancy in these two attitudes? There is

no reason why one should not have a hearty appetite for juicy chops and cream cakes while believing in sorrel for the blood and parsley and pimpernel for the kidneys. But it is a little unusual.

All the more so when one finds her, a year or so later, travelling to the South of France with her friend Irene Dunn, wife of Sir James, becoming obsessed with Yoga after reading *The Garden of Vision* by Adams Beck and determined to 'try out the breathing exercises and the strict vegetarian diet'. Evidently this was easy at Cap Ferrat, but what happened to those juicy chops and not caring a damn about being a bit of a fatty?

On returning from Cap Ferrat Barbara discovers that no less a person than Quaglino ('rapidly becoming the most popular maître d'hôtel, in Mayfair') had named a dish after her. It was called Filet de Truite Barbara Cartland and consisted of a half pound trout covered with a mousseline of sole 'creamed up à l'Anglaise, coated in butter and garnished with stoned grapes and a little Sauce Choron served with Beurre Noisette'.

And then, almost before one stops salivating, she is 'suffering great pain since the good effects of my cure at Brides-les-Bains had worn off' and is off with Irene Dunn to Dr Dengler's sanatorium in Baden-Baden. Everyone was up at six-thirty to climb a mountain before breakfast, drink 'nauseous' Baden salts, endure massage, baths and treatments before compulsory afternoon rest and lights out at ten thirty. Food, minimal, was mainly dry toast and steamed fish. She returned to Dr Dengler three more times and because she was poor he charged a minimal sum.

It was at Baden-Baden that she began to write the first of several books expounding her eclectic personal philosophy. Ronald, her greatest strength, loved it and wrote to tell her that it was 'an inspiration . . . it is a revelation of the person who has shown more courage and virtue in the last two years than most of us can aspire to in a lifetime. God bless you – if you do nothing more you *have* done something now.'

Unfortunately the world thought otherwise. Despite some favourable reviews the book, *Touch the Stars*, sold fewer than five hundred copies, even though her romantic novels were selling more than ten thousand copies each. Inevitably this postponed her emergence as Britain's 'Queen of Health' and as the guru of reincarnation and other relatively unconventional beliefs. This time was yet to come.

Not that she lost interest. In the thirties she met Dr Pierre Lansel who was one of the first doctors in England to practise rejuvenation by administering large quantities of Vitamin B and C (intravenously). He was also a pioneer of hormone treatment. With her friend Lady Rhys-Williams she gave out Vitamin B – in the form of Marmite – to victims of the Depression and also studied the nutritional problems of her brother's constituents in King's Norton. Yoga, too, continued to interest her and she not only practised exercises and breathing with 'the only White Yogi in the world', she wrote a monthly magazine article on the subject.

During the war as County Cadet Officer for the St John's Ambulance Brigade in Bedfordshire she continued to try to make the authorities aware of the importance of nutrition in general and of vitamins in particular. Immediately after the war she was introduced, in the States, to the first B-Complex Multi-Vitamin capsule and introduced it to Britain before the first production company – the Organic Vitamin Company – opened in Hemel Hempstead.

In 1951 she had an almost disastrous experience which fired her enthusiasm for alternative medicine even more. That summer she had a hysterectomy in a private nursing home and everything went wrong. The doctors prescribed morphine to which she was allergic; her haemoglobin count, which should have been between ninety and a hundred, was below forty; they then prescribed Sodium Amytal which proved almost as lethal as the morphine; and there finally came a moment when she 'became aware I was dying'.

An alarmed Hugh did as she demanded – got her out of the nursing home and under the care of their local GP, Dr Kenneth Hutchin, who had been a prisoner of the Japanese in Singapore during the war and knew a thing or two about vitamin deficiency. When she got home she was carried upstairs by the ambulance men to find Dr Hutchin on the landing 'looking like the Statue of Liberty ... with a glass of champagne held high in his hand'. After the restorative champagne he gave her an injection of Vitamin B and continued to do so daily until she made a full recovery. He saved her life.

Now her own household were all put on vitamins and so were the pigs who had Brewer's Yeast from the local brewery and became immensely fertile as a result. When she lectured to Women's Institutes on the marvels of Vitamin B, Miss Cartland used to add one essential caveat. 'One word of warning: I gave Brewer's Yeast to my sows and they all have abnormally large litters.' This invariably caused much merriment.

She had already cured her husband's war-induced bronchitis by feeding him up with honey from the comb (as well as enhancing his sexual performance) and she now returned to promoting her ideas through books. Titles such as *Marriage for Moderns*, *Be Vivid*, *Be Vital*, *Love, Life and Sex* and *Vitamins for Vitality* all propounded the Cartland philosophy. It wasn't, however, until 1960 that she published *The Magic of Honey* which contained the advice, 'Every man who wants to keep well and healthy, and be a good lover should take Honey in the morning and Honey at night. Incidentally I cured my husband of bronchitis by giving him comb-honey for breakfast and comb-honey when he went to bed.'

In support of the sexually enhancing powers of honey she quoted Sir Richard Burton:

> *The Negro Mimun, for full fifty days,*
> *Served numberless girls and gained honour and praise;*
> *And when he was asked to keep it up longer*
> *He did another ten days and finished up stronger!*
> *Now during this test, it was Honey and bread*
> *Enabled his zabzab to hold up its head.*

Honey and bread for the zabzab is an intriguing slogan and also evidence that whatever the moral message of her novels Barbara Cartland has always been a surprisingly sexy authoress, though 'zabzab' is not in any of my dictionaries.

It was in 1964 that she helped to found the National Association for Health of which she later became President. It is on their platform or under their banner that most of her more recent pronouncements have been made. It is as Britain's unofficial Queen of Health also that she sends appropriate gifts to those she thinks might appreciate them. Thus ginseng and stress pills to the Yorkshire and England cricketer Geoffrey Boycott; brain pills (CH_3 Tri-Plus) for a very important person after an unpleasant encounter with a fish-bone – Dame Barbara herself takes two every morning. And so on. The Health Food Industry now, she says, turns over some three hundred million pounds a year and she is, in effect, its spokesman.

She is a particularly apposite figurehead because she is a walking test-bed for health products and her extraordinary nonagenarian energy is a testament to their efficacy. Anyone who is sceptical about such matters has only to look at Dame Barbara.

'Everybody who is really interested in their health', she says, 'should take every day: 2 Healthcrafts Super Vitamin C as a preventative, 1 GEB 6, 2 Gev-E-Tabs and 1 Healthcrafts Vitamin E. Add others if required.'

In 1992 Dame Barbara had another unpleasant experience. She woke one night unable to breathe. Her son was asleep in the next room, gave her a brandy and said she must send for a doctor. She was reluctant but acquiesced. He said she had water on the lung and gave her pills.

Soon afterwards her legs started to be very painful and she went to see the osteopath, Michael Van Straten. He was appalled, administered acupuncture, got Frances Clifford to massage them and gave her some pills from Keith Pollitt which he said would be good for her bones. She was supposed to take four a day but, being her, she took eight, just to be doubly sure of success. They were called 'Porosis' and they seemed to work. Pollitt, incidentally, has another product, Biostrath, which Dame Barbara also swears by.

Some weeks later she was with Joseph Corvo who is a 'Healer' who also practises 'Zone Therapy' on the veins. During the course of their session he suddenly noticed that all the lines on her arms between shoulder and elbow had miraculously disappeared. When she got home Dame Barbara examined her body and found that the same thing had happened. All lines were gone. 'In fact', she claims, 'it was exactly as it was when I was young.'

Dame Barbara insisted that as well as the pills there must be a face cream with similar ingredients. This was duly produced and has worked well not only for Dame Barbara but also for one of her secretaries who used to have dark lines on her neck. After a week of applying the cream these had gone. Dame Barbara made the poor woman show me her neck and I could certainly see no dark lines though as I had not inspected her neck before she began the treatment I was in no position to judge whether or not there had been a change.

'This is all very exciting,' she says, 'as it means that one can go on looking pretty until one is very, very old.' She wanted the cream to be called 'Beauty for Ever' but this was not allowed and the product is now called 'Flame' because of a Goddess called Ayesha who in old age walked through a magic blue flame and was rejuvenated so that she lived on as young and beautiful once more for ever and ever.

As President and Founder of the National Association for Health, Dame Barbara is a walking advertisement for vitamins and Flame and Biostrath and much else besides. Nevertheless I am reminded that her indomitable mother Polly lived to be ninety-eight and in full possession of her powers well into her nineties. It could have as much to do with genetics as with pills.

Nevertheless when it comes to promoting alternative medicines or alternative cosmetics such as those of Princess Shahnaz Husain then Dame Barbara is your woman. There are plenty of conventional doctors and 'experts' who take issue with what she advocates, yet over the years she has as often been proved right as wrong while conventional medicine is looking, by and large, increasingly fallible.

In the end the proof of the pudding is in the eating which is the indestructible Dame Barbara herself and in the many, many letters she receives from satisfied customers.

It also helps that so much of her message is put across in terms so impossible to engage.

'This is a crusade,' she says, 'a crusade against disease and all the evils that attend it. I am convinced that poverty and degradation, war, cruelty and violence all emanate from unhealthy minds dwelling in unhealthy bodies. It is in good health that we are near to the Divine in whose image we have been made.'

Very difficult to argue against someone who is fighting a

crusade against disease; and even if you feel, instinctively, that the answers are not quite as Dame Barbara believes, it is surprisingly difficult to know where and how to begin.

Chapter Sixteen

How Barbara wants to be remembered. But will she? What the cuttings say. The Cartland 'spell' and how it works. She is a bundle of contradictions. She becomes 'the mistress of the soundbite'.

I t is typical of Dame Barbara that every so often she prepares one of her typed volumes bound in dark pink, tied with pink ribbon and entitled, 'How I want to be remembered', or 'How I wish to be remembered'. I have two copies. Off it goes to the newspapers, to television stations, to all the people she thinks should have it. At the *Daily Telegraph* library, where I went to sift through her cuttings, they had lost their copy of 'How I want to be remembered' and were debating how to get hold of another. For some reason their librarian seemed reluctant to approach the Dame direct though I told her she was much the best source. Hugh Massingberd, the obituaries editor, was having her obituary rewritten for the umpteenth time and it seemed appropriate to consider her own wishes in the matter even though they would almost certainly be disregarded, at least in part. I sensed the librarian thought there might be something ghoulish in asking for the booklet direct, but I could be wrong.

There were just the four envelopes devoted to Dame Barbara in the *Telegraph* morgue. The two earliest had been sent over from 'the Warehouse' where really old and redundant records are kept. The relative lack of material seemed to me an indictment of the *Telegraph*'s cutting and filing systems. At Camfield Place there are books and books of cuttings all meticulously logged and stuck in – more than seventy years of national journalism and national celebrity, stretching from the first slightly self-conscious pieces about young girls of today for Lord Beaverbrook in the twenties to reflections on the debutante season of Margaret, Duchess of Argyll in the nineties.

This isn't how she wants to be remembered I reflected as I sat high above the stillborn developments of Docklands and riffled through the dessicated brown newspaper clippings of so many years before. Yet so much of what she wants people to think *has* worked its way into these envelopes. In 1931 someone said 'She is one of the most successful hostesses in London'; in 1935 the *Tatler* wrote that 'The famous author-ess and playwright is a direct descendant of the Dukes of Hamilton and also of Robert the Bruce'; here is the story of her innovative gliding; and a report in *The Times* about her championing the gypsy cause where she is quoted as saying, 'They are British subjects and they have rights.' More recently people have concentrated on her evidently awkward position as step-grandmother to the Princess of Wales and on her relationship with Raine. She is quoted ad nauseam on the subject of the 'hysterical' Princess and her daughter's highly publicised wedding to a French count. This inspired a particularly good *Private Eye* cover with the happy couple posing for the cameras. She is saying, 'You're only marrying me for my mummy.' While he says, 'At last! I'm connected to Royalties!' Early in 1994 she was even given credit for the Prime Minister's controversial initiative, 'Back to Basics'.

There are book reviews, mainly short, not all bad though they tend to get worse with time. There are the little self-deprecating remarks – 'I always wear boot polish on my eyelashes because I am a very emotional person and it doesn't run when I cry.' There is the divorce: 'Cocktails in Bedroom', 'What the butler said'. A 1964 Nicolas Bentley cartoon has a caption saying 'Frankly Aunt Hester, I don't think Barbara Cartland's novels are suitable for grown-ups'.

Tony Palmer went to see her in September 1969 on behalf of John Anstey, the editor of the *Telegraph Sunday Magazine*. Palmer couldn't make her out.

'What a funny mixture she is,' he wrote. 'Kind, generous, witty and yet? Well what? A professional do-gooder? No. A snob? Not really. A bore? Never. Prejudiced? No more than anyone else. Perhaps she's just more honest about herself than the rest of us. Perhaps it *is* true for her, that the plight of the homeless seems to be no more nor less interesting than the fact that during the war Lady Docker kept her jewellery hidden in the cistern of the lavatory.'

That fine journalist, the late Nicholas Tomalin, was similarly perplexed by her 'strange mixture of frilly femininity and steely clinical frankness'. Interviewing her in 1971, for the *Sunday Times*, he, full of plausible manner and rat-like cunning though he was, found himself 'falling with ease into the interrogatory role of a Serena or a Tana who chat with her so winningly in her books'.

Here is Mary Kenny celebrating her eightieth birthday with the notion that 'Underneath all this flim-flam Barbara Cartland is a very substantial character indeed'. Miss Kenny's opinion is that, 'With no background in an age when background counted for everything, with no money in an epoch when money was desperately important and with no natural advantage other than an appetite for relentless work, energy, inventiveness, style and staying-power, she made herself a millionairess and a legend.'

That same year she was interviewed by Jean Rook, the *Daily Express*'s soi-disant 'First Lady of Fleet Street' who became just about her favourite journalist and with whom she shared a strange mixture of romantic almost kitschy schmaltz and ruthless, relentless professionalism. 'I don't mind journalists going on about my pills and my pink frocks and sending me up teasingly because nobody sends up Barbara Cartland better than I do myself,' she told Rook.

I have heard Ian say something similar more than once. I'm not sure it's true but it's a good line of defence. She certainly does it in private. Archie Newman told me how he once asked her to appear at a gala concert to promote her record of romantic love songs with the Royal Philharmonic and she asked him who else would be appearing. When he mentioned Danny la Rue she said 'no'. Newman asked why not. 'Because, darling,' she said, 'the moment I come on no one will know whether it's me or Danny la Rue.'

A marvellously self-deprecating send-up, it's true. But also a very private one. It's not the sort of line that she would allow herself in public. At least I don't think so. And because of that the public, particularly the chattering-class sort of public, tend to take her at face value and assume that she takes herself more seriously than, privately, she sometimes does.

There is something depressing about these dead brown envelopes, particularly in Canary Wharf in deepest Dock-lands, this failed dream of a place. When Dame Barbara and the century were young the London docks would have been teeming with life and activity with ships and cargoes from every part of the world. Now it is a half-completed, half-empty building site; the *Telegraph* journalists sit here staring at their screens like the last survivors of some terminal catastrophe, cut off from the recognisable world – certainly from any world Dame Barbara would recognise.

The newspapers and the publishers for whom she works, as well as the people with whom she plays, used to be in the centre of town. Now they are dispersed. The newspapers have abandoned Fleet Street; the publishers have deserted Bloomsbury; Mayfair and Belgravia is all flats or embassies. Her world is dead and yet, like some gallant old brigantine, she sails on through the nineties, seeming not to recognise that life is no longer what it was.

Some of the cuttings are so old that they crumble in my hands like shreds of tobacco from a dry cigar. I stuff them back in their envelopes and hand them in at the desk. The earlier two packets will go back to the warehouse and the others will remain here at Canary Wharf ready for the next person who wants to write about her. In a sense this *is* how she will be remembered. Not for nothing is the collective name for the files of personal cuttings 'the morgue'. In the end, even for the great and the good, it is not so much dust to dust and ashes to ashes as lifeblood to newsprint and vitality to column inches. You cannot cram a real person into brown envelopes and then reduce them into a few inches of obituary. And yet we do and the day will come when just such a fate will come even to Dame Barbara, so that she will be 'Dame Barbara Cartland who died yesterday was . . .' And then there will be two or three thousand words of dubious facts and contentious opinions.

However, by the time she dies her own 'How I want to be remembered' should be in the files as well. It is a curious document, partly, I think – and this seems to me one of the central problems with Dame Barbara – because it is essentially meant for public consumption. Therefore, I submit, she is telling the world how she *ought* to be remembered, which is not quite the same thing. She once said to me at Camfield that 'Of course, darling, one can't tell the truth' and I know what she meant. Yet so often she seems to think that a sanitised, romanticised version of herself is more appealing than the real her. I don't think she is right, though perhaps in a commercial sense she is. Perhaps the books wouldn't sell if her readers didn't believe 'How I want to be remembered'.

The document runs to twenty-five pages in all, but she has numbered the particular achievements with which she wants to be identified. In the first of the documents I have, she lists them as follows:

1 The books, especially the novels.
2 The Aeroplane-towed Glider.
3 Being gazetted an Honorary Junior Commander in the ATS and the only Lady Welfare Officer in Bedfordshire.
4 Being made a Dame of Grace of the Order of St John of Jerusalem.
5 Being a Conservative Member of Hertfordshire County Council.
6 Founding the National Association for Health.
7 Recording her album of Romantic Love Songs with the Royal Philharmonic Orchestra.
8 Being chosen as 'Achiever of the Year' by the National Home Furnishing Association of Colorado Springs.
9 Being voted, in 1983, 'Best-Dressed Woman in the World' by Bill Bass.
10 Being given La Medaille de la Ville de Paris.
11 Being asked by Rajiv Gandhi to open a Health Resort outside Delhi.

That was the list after she had written 475 books. After 525 books she amended it so that getting the law of England changed so that gypsy children could go to school became number twelve. At number thirteen she added being published in Poland and the Arab world 'because I am moral'.

Being made a Dame – a proper one, not a Dame of St John – in the 1991 New Year's Honours List comes in as a sort of PS but is not dignified with a number. This award, incidentally, was for all-round public services, not for 'services to literature'. How and why it finally happened is, as always with these things, a grand secret but there are persistent rumours among Cartland watchers that it owed much to a direct intervention from the Queen Mother herself.

It is a peculiar list in a number of ways. Perhaps by reducing it to its essentials I have made it look more ridiculous than it really is. I simply cannot believe, for instance, that even in a mood of seriously perverse aberration the Dame could possibly want to be remembered more for opening an Indian health spa – even at Rajiv Gandhi's behest – than for being the mother of Raine. Surely she must value her lifetime of highly opinionated journalism more than being given a gold medal by the Mayor of Paris?

And yet.

The gold medal from Jacques Chirac celebrated twenty-five million copies of her novels being translated into French, 'creating', she said, 'a great deal of employment' not to mention (which she doesn't) a great deal of cash for Cartland Promotions.

When she went to Paris to receive her gong her publishers paid a million francs for an hour of television. She had a 'charming' interviewer and Charles Aznavour sang. The studio was thick with pink roses and she was showered with pink rose petals from the ceiling.

Then, in her own inimitable words: 'After the interview I was taken outside and sat in an open Rolls Royce in the Park where, by permission of the Prime Minister, pink fireworks were exploded above my head. The initials 'B.C.' were entwined with a heart and others were great bursts of pink roses.

'I believe it was the first time such a tribute had been paid to an Author.'

There is sometimes a quite touching naivety about the

Dame, all the more so, I think, because she is in so many ways such a canny, world-weary old article.

'I believe it was the first time such a tribute had been paid to an Author.'

Perhaps I am being unduly cynical if I say I do not entirely believe 'How I want to be remembered'. I don't mean that it's entirely false, though it is in some measure part of the Cartland publicity machine and a degree of suspicion is therefore healthy. I do mean that it is a public document reflecting public aspirations. Some of these may indeed be near to the Cartland heart but I do not believe they really tell the truth, the whole truth and nothing but the truth.

The question is probably an impossible one for anyone to answer with absolute honesty. Indeed the only genuine answer must surely be that all of us wish to be remembered as being more wonderful than we are. We do not wish our sins and misdemeanours, perhaps least of all our smaller vices, to be found out even when we are dead. Conversely, we would welcome a few posthumously recognised virtues to which we could not pretend in real life. The fact that Dame Barbara has issued her pre-emptive strike against the obituarists is interesting if only as an indication, if one were needed, that she is intensely conscious of the image she presents to the world. I remain unconvinced about the contents, but then only a saint, and perhaps not even a saint, could produce such a statement with absolute honesty.

I know that I shall remember her with affection. There are things in this book which I know she would prefer me not to have written. Having said that, I like to think that there is very little with which she would not have some private sympathy. Her objections lie in my having the temerity to say these things out loud.

As I have tried to demonstrate, however, the truth about Barbara Cartland is much more interesting and sympathetic than the received image. The fact that we have received this image because it is the one she has tried to project does not make this any the less true.

During the months of my research I, like John Pearson and Gwen Robyns before me, became very fond of the Dame. I'm not unusual in this. In her interview with Anthony Clare she claimed that even in her nineties she was able to make many men fall in love with her. I deny being in love with Dame Barbara. After all I am over forty years her junior; but I don't deny being fond and what's more, becoming fonder the better I felt I was getting to know her. And it's clear that she has the same effect on many men she knows at all well.

Affection like this defies a totally rational analysis but I know that almost top of my list of reasons would be vulnerability. I remember once being met at Hatfield railway station by Dame Barbara's lady's maid. She dropped me at the front door of Camfield Place. It was unlocked and I walked into the hall without ringing the bell. As I entered, Dame Barbara also entered left from the door which led to the secretaries' office. She was wearing the usual pink, this time a mildly diaphanous sort of tent, and the mask of make-up was in place. Such trouble, such attention to detail and style, for an ordinary day of dictation and a chat with the biographer.

For months now she had been grumbling to me about her failing eyesight. Not whingeing, not what she referred to in her interview with Anthony Clare as 'that *stupid* sadness', but a characteristically robust grumble about the sheer maddening inconvenience of losing your sight. It was a nuisance not being able to see properly. The staff had to enlarge pages of print that she wanted to read. It seemed to be getting worse.

Now for a moment Dame Barbara seemed fazed in a way I had never seen before. You could hardly blame her. She had heard the door open and close but she *couldn't see who it was*. She was in her nineties, *on her own*. The dogs were not in sight. Likewise the staff. It could have been a thief in a balaclava with a sawn-off shotgun or a mad rapist released into the community from some psychiatric hospital at the behest of Mrs Bottomley. It was perfectly normal for her to seem apprehensive.

And that's my point. Until then I had believed in the mask and the armour; I really did think that nothing could dent her invincibility. Now, just for a moment, I had a glimpse of a little old lady all on her own and, even, slightly frightened. It passed in a second because I stuttered out an apologetic 'Hello, it's only me' and there was instant recovery, a kiss on both cheeks, and one was virtually frogmarched on to the sofa in the drawing-room. All confidence was restored but I felt that for a second I had seen what that indomitable appearance concealed.

Most of us like a fighter and it is a mistake to think that the Cartland success has come easily or naturally. Nor should one believe that the superiority she assumes in public appearances and interviews are as effortless as they seem. There has been an enormous amount of hard work and of courage.

'We've all got knocks,' she said, from the psychiatrist's chair. 'We've all had terrible things happening – you tell me anyone who hasn't. But you've got to learn to be strong and to be proud and stand up to it. You've got to learn that the world isn't all softness and sweetness but you're meant to develop yourself and develop your mind by fighting the things that you think are wrong or are wrong for you. If you don't fight for the world, you fight for yourself. Of course you do.'

For someone who has apparently had such a lifelong yen to find a strong man into whose arms she could dissolve she has not had much luck. Her father sounds weak and she hardly knew him in the crucial teenage years when she was growing up. Then he was killed just when he might have been of most use. The women, Barbara and her mother Polly, were bereft but also abandoned and let down.

Ronald was, in many ways, the love of her life: 'everything together except for sex.' The intensity of that sibling relationship must have been difficult for any conventional suitor to cope with. He was her prop at the most difficult time of her life. He was also, in the words of his admirer, Lord Deedes, 'The genuine article'. Had he not died at Dunkirk might he not have guarded his sister from the excesses of pink and self-publicity which have sometimes made her a public figure of fun? Arguable at least.

Her first husband, Sachie, was clearly a weak man. The image of him being sent away to preparatory school unable even to dress himself, putting shoes on the wrong feet, mocked and derided and bullied in the peculiarly feline manner of little boys in boarding schools, is a pathetic one. No wonder he took to drink. No wonder he took to the strong, dominating matron-like figure of Barbara. But why she him? Is it because while part of her has a need to fall at the feet of the master of her fate she also has a corresponding need to be a mother figure? In the case of Sachie it seems a logical explanation.

And Hugh? After the trauma and scandal of so public a divorce she was happily married to Hugh for over a quarter of a century. Hugh was charming and comfortable, romantic when occasion demanded. Exciting? Dominant? I don't think so. Truth be told he sounds quite happy to play second fiddle to his remarkable spouse. Comfortable but not the stuff of a Cartland hero.

Which, of course, is what Lord Mountbatten was. Mountbatten had strength and heroics in buckets. In her mind she turned him into a classic Cartland hero. Then he too was removed from her life in the same violent way as her father and her two brothers.

That's a lot of loss even for a woman who has lived a life as long as Dame Barbara's. It would be bizarre if there were not scars as a result. Not that it has made her any the less besotted with the opposite sex. She has gone on adoring men all her life, made no secret of much preferring her sons Ian and Glen to her difficult daughter Raine. She finds women difficult while, paradoxically, founding her fortune on writing books for them.

Odd.

Today Dame Barbara turns up in the most unexpected places and guises. The Oriental in Bangkok, for instance. This hotel prides itself on its literary connections and has named suites after the distinguished authors who have 're-sided' there.

Bound copies of their work can be found in antique Thai bookcases at the entrance to the Authors' lounge and they include those well known Far East hands, Joseph Conrad, Somerset Maugham, Noël Coward and Graham Greene as well as the Dame herself.

'During a recent sojourn at The Oriental,' says the glossy brochure, 'she began writing a romance based in Thailand at the turn of the century. It is titled *Journey to a Star*.'

For those contemplating a stay in the Barbara Cartland Suite this is what to expect: 'The living-room is a harmony of salmon floor coverings, grey-on-white fabrics contrasting with deep-stained woods and a beautifully glass-panelled library case. The bedroom features floral oil paintings hung on gentle floral wall coverings. Pastel quilted bedcovers and richly stained, ornately carved bedhead.'

It may be Bangkok but it certainly sounds as if it owes something to her own dear Camfield Place.

Very Barbara Cartland.

She is still a bundle of contradictions: strong yet vulnerable; romantic and fluffy yet aggressive and bossy; a rattling box full of daily pills and vitamins yet a regular taker of afternoon tea with cream cakes and meringues. 'Common' and 'vulgar' are some of the worst things she could say about someone and yet those are words that her more snobbish enemies regularly use about her. 'Limp' is another.

Ultimately, however, the verdict on Dame Barbara must be that however maddening and ridiculous she sometimes seems she is always one of the greatest life-enhancers. Few people in a drab century for her country contributed more to the gaiety of the British nation.

It is perhaps symptomatic that in later life she has given up any very serious attempt to write better books than other people but settled instead for writing more. As she has grown older, so her energy has seemed to increase. She is unstoppable and she is everywhere. Every journalist in Britain, stumped for a spark of colour to illuminate a story on anything with the slightest social or romantic connotation, turns to her and she always obliges not only with noblesse but with skill and wit. She made herself the mistress of the soundbite before anyone knew what a soundbite was.

Considering any colourful or unusual figure there is a temptation to use phrases such as 'after God created Dame Barbara he threw away the mould' or 'We shall not see her like again' or simply 'She was a phenomenon'.

Barbara Cartland never has been simply the top of a class; she was always distinct from any class or group. It's true that she is the most prolific romantic novelist of all time but she is not like any other romantic novelist. Her punditry is completely distinctive. Her appearance likewise. As Frances Whitehead at Mills and Boon remarked: 'A generic.'

All her life has been devoted to inventing herself. No one else could have conceived such a person or constructed her with such skill, devotion and exuberance. In the end it's sad perhaps that the sum of her achievements is less than the sum of herself.

'How I want to be remembered' is a list which never quite measures up to the person who created it. Any objective assessment must surely be that however she may wish to be remembered, Barbara Cartland will long be remembered for being Barbara Cartland.

Chapter Seventeen

A final word from Barbara on the final subject – 'Where I want to be buried'. She threatens to return after death.

During one of her phone calls Dame Barbara warned me that if I wrote things she didn't like she'd come back and haunt me. I am afraid that I *have* written words she won't like though not maliciously so. I like and admire her but I have tried to be honest, which can be painful. I also find it difficult not to risk an affectionate tease from time to time. She invites it. As Philip Ziegler says, 'She's a card.'

I rather hope she does come and haunt me, wreathed in a pink concoction by Worth or Hardy Amies with a cerise halo in place of one of those hats. She'd make a fabulous ghost and cheer me up no end. She seems to believe in a form of Buddhist reincarnation so will be putting in some sort of reappearance on this earth in any case. I just hope I'm on her visiting list.

Meanwhile, I feel she ought to have the last word: 'I was absolutely furious with the local bishop,' she said, during that delicious creamy lunch. The bishop had told her that long inscriptions were no longer to be allowed on gravestones, that they had to lie flush with the grass so as not to interfere with the man doing the mowing, and they couldn't be made of marble because that would last too long.

'So I rang the local vicar', she said, 'and I told him I'm going to be buried in the garden. We'll have a service and you can come and tell me about it. But if I can't have a decent tomb I shall be buried in the garden.'

Index